*Angels singi'*

# HEAVEN

## *For a Home with God*

*What on Earth are you doing for Heaven's sake?*

*TED talk*

Steve Klein & Jeff May

*Job "Do you think I should answer you," according to your sense of justice?*

HEAVEN: *O For a Home with God*
Copyright © 2014 Steve Klein & Jeff May
All rights reserved
ISBN 978-0-692-32570-4

# Dedication

*To our wives, Sandi Klein and Susan May,*
*our companions and loving supporters*
*on our journey to a home with God.*

# *Acknowledgments*

*Cover Photo: Wayne Holt*
*Proofreading: Shirley Holt*

# Foreword

Heaven. We sing about it. We hear sermons about it. We know the Bible holds it before us as our ultimate goal. But in the hustle and bustle of life, we tend to give little thought to heaven, and we might even have difficulty seeing it as a reality. There are so many distractions. To mention jobs, our obsession with sports, demands from our family, checking our messages, community service, vacations, weekend trips, and caring for elderly parents is only to begin a list of distractions. As a result, our lives can become earth-centered rather than heaven-centered, and our affections too often are placed on earthly things rather than on things above.

Steve Klein and Jeff May jolt us into seeing heaven as a reality. They take us from the shattered dreams of this life to the place where there are no shattered dreams, from the wicked surroundings of this world to the realm where all is pure and holy, from the suffering we experience in this life to that life where there will be no suffering, from a place of tears to a place where there will be no more tears, from dying to living, from the temporal to the eternal, to the very dwelling place of God, to the place where we shall see our Lord, to the realm where for the first time we will fully realize what He did for us, and "falling on our knees," give to Him the praise He truly deserves, praise which we so inadequately give to Him today.

There we shall join the innumerable company of angels and all the redeemed around the throne, worshipping Him who is on the throne and the Lamb forever and ever. There we will experience no boredom, no "wishing for elsewhere to be," but only joy and peace and love. In this life we struggle with temptations, but there we will be free of all temptations. Steve and Jeff, using the scriptures, bring us to long for that city.

This book reminds us of the value of heaven as seen in all that God did in making it possible for us to be saved, cleansed, justified, and fitted for that abode. We are also reminded that while our hope is in God's grace and love, we must take up our cross and follow our Lord if we are to find comfort and assurance in that hope.

Steve and Jeff do not avoid passages that have disputed interpretations, passages such as John 14:1-3 and Revelation, chapter 21. You may agree or disagree with their interpretation, but if you read this book with a critical eye you will miss out on the picture of beauty, grandeur, and joy to which it directs our attention.

Finally, we express our thanks to Steve and Jeff, men who by their lives and teaching demonstrate their hope of being in that home about which they have written. Read, think, meditate, dream, live, hope, and praise God. May we hear the Lord say through His grace, "Well done."

-- *Bill Hall*

# *Contents*

## CHAPTER 6: Conformed to the Image of His Son
(Steve Klein)

## CHAPTER 7: Living a Heavenly Life on Earth
(Steve Klein)

## CHAPTER 8: Working to be Rewarded
## and Remembered (Steve Klein)

## CHAPTER 9: Help from Heaven
(Jeff May)

## CHAPTER 10: Hindrances & Obstacles
(Jeff May)

*Chapter One*

# $\mathcal{H}$eaven: God's Eternal Home

I was on my computer when it happened.  A news flash simply read, *"Mine Rescue Begins In Chile."*  I knew it was coming, but it caught me off guard.  Who didn't know this story?  It had captivated millions around the world since it happened.  I ran downstairs, turned on the news, and there I saw him.

Seven-year-old Barion Avelos stood wiping tears of joyful anticipation. His eyes were fixed on the 28-inch opening of a rescue shaft that plummeted to a depth of 2300 feet.  That's almost twice the height of the Empire State Building!  There entombed in the bowels of the earth was his father Florencio, the miner chosen to be the first to ride in a capsule that would lift him to the earth's surface.

I tried to read every emotion on this son's face. I wondered what this little boy's thoughts had been at bedtime all the previous nights.  Is my dad going to be okay?  Will I ever see him again?  Could there be another landslide that will bury him forever?

Eighteen minutes must have felt like eternity while Barion waited.   And then in a moment it happened!  His father surfaced; Barion saw his face and ran into the arms of his father.  Millions, and I too, cried tears of joy.  Maybe because it was some good news in the world for a change.

It didn't take long for it to click in my mind that this was sort of a modern-day parable, an earthly story packed with heavenly meaning.  For as great as the emotions of this day were for young Barion and others who would soon see their fathers, it could not

possibly touch the delight of the day when I finally see my
heavenly Father and my Lord Jesus!  That day is coming, you
know.  All of God's children anticipate it with great longing.

> "Beloved, now we are the children of God, and it has not
> yet been revealed what we shall be, but we know that
> when He is revealed, we shall be like Him,
> for *we shall see Him as He is.*"
> (1 John 3:2)

God is what makes heaven, heaven.  It is where He is.  Heaven
without God is a contradiction of terms.  Heaven is so linked with
God, the words are often used synonymously.  When the prodigal
son returned home, his words were, *"Father, I have sinned against
heaven"* (Luke 15:18).  To sin against heaven is to sin against God.

Jesus often reminded us that heaven is God's eternal home.
The model prayer even begins, "Our Father, which art in heaven"
(Matt. 6:9).  Fifteen times in Matthew, Jesus will speak of the
Father "in heaven."  Sometimes it sounds much like an address.
He is the Lord God *of* heaven (Gen. 24:7), just as I am Jeff May of
Athens.  It has always been God's home, His "holy habitation"
(Deut. 26:15).

His home is not where the birds fly, or where the sun, moon,
and stars are set.  His home is called by Paul, the third heaven
(2 Cor. 12:2-4).  It is a spiritual place, not a physical one.  Perhaps
this is why Soviet leader Nikita Khrushchev missed it when he said
of his country's cosmonaut, "Gagarin flew into space, but didn't see
any God there."  He was looking too low.  Actually he wasn't
looking at all!

This is not to say that God is not everywhere.  The Bible is
clear that God is omnipresent, and He has left divine fingerprints
all over the created world.  There is no excuse for missing the
evidence of His existence (Rom. 1:20).  Solomon said it well after
building the temple of God, "Behold, heaven and the heaven of
heavens cannot contain You.  How much less, this house that I
have built" (1 Kings 8:27)!  How do you contain such greatness?
It would be like trying to press all the air in the world into a Mason
jar.  But nevertheless, heaven is His home, the center of His
operations.  This is why Solomon continued to say, "When they

2

pray toward this place, then hear in heaven Your dwelling place" (1 Kings 8:30).

## BEAUTIFUL BEYOND WORDS

Of course heaven will be a place of beauty. Would we expect anything else at God's house? We know beauty here below: the Grand Canyon, Niagara Falls, the Northern Lights, etc. And this is a place where God puts His feet, His footstool (Acts 7:49). What must His throne room look like? Scripture has a number of symbolic visions of heaven which seek to capture the beauty, holiness, and majesty of being in God's presence (Rev. 4:1-11; 7:9-12; Isa. 6:1-3; Dan. 7:9-10). I am convinced that heaven's beauty is a hard thing to capture in writing. Human language limits us too much, but those who wrote, by the Spirit's inspiration, did the best that can be done. How do you describe a place of spiritual beauty with physical words? Let's just say for now that it is a place of breathtaking and dazzling beauty and glory. Those who saw it responded in awe and reverence. Don't let symbolic language make you think it is not real. Heaven is the most real thing there is. Only the unseen things are eternal (2 Cor. 4:18). When symbolic language is used in the Bible, it always means that something *very important* is being discussed.

I look forward to such an awesome place of beauty, but it is the icing on the cake. If God is not there, it is just a place. Something is wrong with our thinking if we become materialistic in our thinking about heaven. We sing the song, "I'm satisfied with just a cottage below, a little silver, a little gold (aren't we in pitiful shape?), but in that city where the ransomed will shine, I want a gold one that's silver lined." Is that as high as our aspirations are about heaven?

Think with me. In Acts chapter one, the apostles stand listening to Jesus as He speaks His final earthly words. He finishes speaking, and as they look, His feet begin to lift off the ground, then He is head high, and then He is a speck ascending in the clouds. The disciples stood there gazing into heaven, and angels appeared saying, "Why do you stand gazing into heaven?" They assured them He would be back. At that moment, why do you think they wanted to go to heaven? The answer is simple. It is

3

where HE is! God is the centerpiece of heaven. If you have ever taken a loved one to the airport to say goodbye for an extended time, you probably can relate to the feeling of the apostles when Jesus left them. You also likely stood there gazing into the clouds until the plane that carried your loved one became a small dot, and then disappeared.

Yes, we will enjoy the beauty of heaven because of the beauty of the One who prepared it. But someone has said, "Thinking only of streets of gold and pearly gates with no mention of the Lord is about like a bride who goes on and on about her silverware and fine china yet never says a word about the bridegroom." Something is missing, don't you think? Listen to the Psalmist.

> *"Whom have I in heaven but You?*
> *And there is none upon earth*
> *that I desire besides You."*
> (Ps. 73:25)

I am so thankful God has prepared a place of beauty for us. He didn't have to make His home, our home. But even if it wasn't a place of beauty, "Anywhere is home, if Christ, my Lord, is there."

## GOD'S GREAT DREAM

Making heaven our home was God's dream for us from before the creation of the world. I remember my great dreams when my wife and I were planning a family. I had so much love in my heart that I wanted to share with my children. I wanted to give them a place to long for, come to, and feel secure. Who doesn't like a warm fire in the hearth, a couch, and a blanket with loved ones nearby? Does it get much better? That's what home is. For most of us, the word "home" stirs all sorts of warm emotions. I still remember an episode of Little House on the Prairie where Laura Ingalls says, "Home is the nicest word there is."

It seems this must have been what God wanted. Because God is love (1 John 4:8), and had so much love in His heart, He decided to enlarge His family. He had a Son, but He wanted to lead many sons to glory (Heb. 2:10). His dream is to one day pour out all of His kindness on us.

> *"...that in the ages to come He might show*
> *the exceeding riches of His grace*
> *in His kindness toward us in Christ Jesus."*
> (Eph. 2:6-7)

What a dream! But oh, how it would cost Him! While the Bible does not give all the details, the plan was conceived in the mind of God to make man. Then comes the problem of realizing man would sin. God can't live with sinners, and the penalty for sin is death. Should He make them pay the death penalty once they sin? Somewhere in eternity past, Jesus agreed to pay the penalty, to die for us. Now folks, that's love!! God didn't have to make us. He knew what it would cost Him. Yet, He did it anyway. That's all I have to know to realize that heaven must be wonderful beyond my wildest imagination. Jesus died to give us a shot at it! Enough said.

This plan of salvation was more beautiful than we could have ever fathomed. Paul says, "Eye has not seen, nor ear heard, nor have entered into the heart of man the things which God has prepared for those who love Him" (1 Cor. 2:9). We only know the plan because God has now revealed it. I love the words of Paul Earnhart, who in a sermon said, "This plan was not something God drew up on a Saturday afternoon when He had nothing else to do."

In Romans 8:29-30, two verses say volumes in unfolding the dream.

> *"For whom He foreknew, He also predestined to be*
> *conformed to the image of His Son, that He might*
> *be the firstborn among many brethren.*
> *Moreover whom He predestined, these He also called,*
> *whom He called, these He also justified,*
> *and whom He justified, these He also glorified."*

See the process? God **predetermined to have a family**. All of the family must **take on the character of the original Son, Jesus**. He would **issue a call** to these people by preaching the

5

gospel to draw them out of the world. The gospel will then cut into every society, dividing people into two groups: those who want it, and those who don't. Those who respond to heaven's invitation by obeying the gospel are **justified** (set free from the death penalty), and at last **glorified**. Glorification is a journey. God, little by little, works to transform us into the likeness of His Son. I tell you, that's glory (2 Cor. 3:18)! Each little bit we become like Jesus is so glorious. While here below, we cooperate with the Spirit of God to take on the traits of the heavenly family, and at the last God caps it off by making us just like Jesus (1 John 3:2-3). I call this, THE PROGRAM. And indeed, we need to "get with the program."

## EVERYBODY WANNA GO TO HEAVEN?

Because heaven is so wonderful, it is hard to understand why so few yearn for it? Country music artist Kenny Chesney sings, "Everybody wanna go to heaven, but nobody wanna go now." Hank Williams Jr. sings, "If heaven ain't a lot like Dixie, I don't want to go" and then adds "Just send me to hell or New York City, it would be about the same to me." Billy Joel pens the words, "They say there's a heaven for those who will wait. Some say its better but I say it ain't. I'd rather laugh with the sinners than cry with saints. The sinners are much more fun. You know that only the good die young." How God must hurt to have invested all He had to give us a dreamland and so many treat it with outright mockery. How ungrateful can we be?

Someone once said, "Heaven must first be in us, before we are in heaven." It is for those who themselves dream about it and stay focused on the pursuit of it. It seems the majority of people realize there is going to be a crash one day (the world will end), and then there will be two chutes we can slide down. One leads to heaven and the other leads to hell. Given those two options, they'll choose heaven. That's a no-brainer. But that's about all the thought that is given to it and don't expect some folks to devote much more mental energy to it before that day. Such meager thoughts about heaven will not get us there. There's an old spiritual which says, "Everybody thinking about heaven ain't going there." It is a **prepared place** for a **prepared people**.

Even Christians sometimes say things that are disturbing to me. Like the story that is sometimes told about a preacher who asked from the pulpit, "Everyone who wants to go to heaven, raise your hand." Everyone raised their hands except brother Jones. So the preacher called once again. Brother Jones still didn't raise his hand. The preacher said, "Brother Jones, don't you want to go to heaven?" Brother Jones replied, "Oh yes. I want to go to heaven, but I thought you were getting up a busload to go now."

Then there is a fairly common response when we ask, "How are you doing today?" Someone will say, "It's a good day. Any day above the ground is a good day. It beats the alternative." Does it really? Being in paradise would surely beat anything here below, wouldn't it? Where is the longing, the anticipation? Why wouldn't we want to go *now*?

Let's contrast the above sentiments with that of the apostle Paul, who said, *"O, Lord come"* (1 Cor. 16:22). Or what about John who wrote, "He who testifies to these things says, 'Surely, I am coming quickly.' Amen. *Even so, come Lord Jesus"* (Rev. 22:20).

Now, I understand there can be a bit of a tension here. There can be good reason in our minds to stay here longer, but it is not so that we can go shopping again, play more golf, catch the next ballgame, or head to the woods for another hunt or a good fishin' hole. Paul felt a tug from both worlds. In prison, with a possible death penalty looming, he wrote, "For I am hard pressed between the two, having a desire to depart and be with Christ, which is far better. Nevertheless to remain in the flesh is more needful for you" (Phil. 1:23-24). His only reason for desiring to stay was to continue to bless others spiritually. Beyond that, He was eager to go on! Are we? Heaven's people are eagerly waiting for Jesus' coming (Phil. 3:20; 1 Cor. 1:7). They set their affections on it (Col. 3:1-4). They look for it and want it to hurry up and arrive (2 Pet. 3:12).

People all about us are longing for satisfaction and searching for meaning and purpose, but they seek for them in the counterfeits: money, materialism, prestige, recreation, and sex. Oh, these things will offer some moment of pleasure but it will not last. Just ask Moses (Heb. 11:24-27) or Solomon (Eccl. 2:1-11). Solomon had the means to have it all. He had unlimited access and resources. Yet, he said he found nothing satisfying. People still come up empty.

What is it we are all longing for? What is the itch that cries out to be scratched? It is **eternity with God**! He has placed eternity in our hearts (Eccl. 3:11). People may not realize where their search for purpose is intended to end, but that's where it is. Just as a fish could never be happy out of water, and just as an eagle was made to soar in the sky, we will never be happy apart from God. We were made by Him and for Him (Col. 1:16). Solomon concluded that serving God is the "whole of man" (Eccl. 12:13-14). To pursue anything else leads out into nothingness.

## DREAMING THE HOURS AWAY

Are you in the company of people who dream of heaven? I remember once having a brother in Christ who told me of an occasion when he was heavy in meditation about heaven. He said, "After a while, a feeling came to me. I felt a little strange. Then I realized the feeling I was having was the feeling you get when you are homesick." That's not weird. This ought to be the feeling of all of God's people.

We are in the strange land. Heaven is where our home is (Phil. 3:20). If we have truly come to know God and have come to know Jesus, both by reading about Him and experiencing Him in life, why wouldn't we feel homesick? Those before us have.

"These all died in faith, not having received
the promises but having seen them afar off
were *assured of them, embraced them* and confessed
that they were *strangers and pilgrims* on the earth.
For those who say such things declare plainly
that *they seek a homeland."*
(Heb. 11:13-14)

"But now *they desire a better, that is a heavenly country.*
Therefore God is not ashamed to be called their God,
for *He has prepared a city for them."*
(Heb. 11:16)

Let's set our sights on heaven. It's not true that we can be "so heavenly-minded that we are of no earthly good." Jesus' zeal for heaven and God's work was so great that His own people said, "He is out His mind" (Mark 3:21). Truth is, He is the sanest person who ever walked on earth. We are the ones living in the insane asylum. Those who do the greatest good for earth are those who are so minded to think like Him. Let God teach you how to treasure heaven in your heart. This is where we intend to journey in this book. Will you join us?

Heaven. God dreams it for us. Let's do the same. Can you identify with the words of this old hymn where the writer dreams the hours away? I hope you can.

> *Closing my eyes at eve and thinking of heaven's grace,*
> *Longing to see my Lord, yes, meeting Him face to face;*
> *Trusting Him as my all wheresoever my footsteps roam,*
> *Pleading with Him to guide me on to the Spirit's home.*
>
> *O! for a home with God, a place in His courts to rest,*
> *Sure in a safe abode with Jesus and the blest;*
> *Rest for a weary soul, once redeemed by the Savior's love,*
> *Where I'll be pure and whole and live with my God above!*

Home. Those trapped miners in Chile thought of little else. It only makes sense that we do the same. Their rescuers did not have to show such mercy. Neither did God in saving us. We certainly didn't deserve it. I marvel that He would even set His mind on me (Ps. 8:3-5). He is so great. I am so small (Isa. 40). And yet He thinks about me and you more times than can be numbered (Ps. 139:17-18). His family is important to Him. We are the reason everything was created in the first place. And at every point in the history of this world, we are at the center of His will and His purpose. Shouldn't we think more about Him? Let's go home. There's no place like it.

## QUESTIONS

1.  In what ways are heaven and God connected in Scripture?

2.  Using 2 Cor. 4:18, how would you answer someone who says of heaven, "If I can't see it or touch it, I don't believe in it"?

3.  What should we desire the most about heaven - the things that are there or the One who is there?  Explain your answer.

4.  Using Eph. 1:5 and other passages in this chapter, why did God create us and prepare heaven for us?  Are you glad He did?  Explain.

5.  Study Romans 8:29-30 carefully.  List the things God desires to do for all of us.

6.  **Thought Question**:  Why do you think so many people don't express much desire for spiritual things or for heaven?

7.  How do God's children feel about heaven?  Support your answer with Scriptures cited in this lesson and others you may know.

8.  **Thought Question:**  What might help us to long for heaven more than we often do?

*Chapter Two*

# *J*esus Christ
## – Trailblazer to Heaven

**On September 11, 2001**, as the passengers of United
Flight 93 began to realize that their hijackers did not intend for
them to live, many made desperate attempts to contact loved ones.
Using air phones and cell phones, calls were made to wives,
husbands, mothers, and sisters. Other passengers, not able to reach
family members, left messages with phone operators and on
answering machines. Thirty-seven calls were made in the minutes
before the airliner plunged into that field in Pennsylvania. Whom
would you have called?

On the night of His betrayal, when Jesus knows that His death
is near, He too reaches out to a loved One. He makes several
fervent requests of His Father that evening; some in Gethsemane,
and some as He prayed with His disciples earlier in the upper
room. One such appeal to His Father is found in John 17:5, where
He prays, "And now, O Father, glorify Me together with Yourself,
with the glory which I had with You before the world was."

## AT HOME BEFORE THE WORLD BEGAN

In the face of death, it is said that your entire life can flash
before your eyes in a moment. As Jesus faced His darkest hour,
His mind journeyed back through time, back beyond His earthly
life, across centuries and centuries, and into the epoch of eternity

11

before time itself began. There He had been with His Father in glory. And there He longed to be again. With His mind firmly fixed on going back home, all that He was to suffer in the hours ahead could be borne. Indeed, it was "for the joy that was set before Him" that He "endured the cross, despising the shame, and has sat down at the right hand of the throne of God" (Heb. 12:2).

The Scriptures reveal little about the life of God's Son before He came to earth. From John 1:1, we learn that "He was in the beginning with God." The few references that He makes while on earth to that earlier existence seem to center around being in the presence of His Father. In John 16:28 He says, "I came forth from the Father and have come into the world. Again, I leave the world and go to the Father." Even when He tells us about the "many mansions" in the heavenly realm, He connects them to the dwelling of His Father – "In my Father's house are many mansions" (John 14:2).

And in His Father's house, before the world began, there was love between Father and Son. Jesus shares the memory of that love with His Father when He prays, "You loved Me before the foundation of the world" (John 17:24). Attempting to fathom the depth and intensity of the love that is shared between two divine Persons stretches the limits of human comprehension. But there, in His Father's house before the foundation of the world, the Son of God had known it.

## LEAVING HOME

Do you remember the day you left your parents' home to make your way in the world? Maybe you were heading off to college, or starting a new job, or had just gotten married. If you were close to your parents, leaving the comfort and love of home was probably difficult, especially if that is all you had ever known.

Jesus left a home filled with light and love to enter a world of darkness. The change in circumstances and in apparent status could not have been more dramatic. It has been compared to a human allowing himself to be transformed into a dog and living and dying as a dog in order to save the canine world. What human would do it? Yet the gap between living as God and living as man is surely infinitely greater than the difference between living as a man and living as an animal. Jesus existed in the form of God, but He took on the form of a servant. He enjoyed the highest standing in heaven and earth, yet He made Himself of no reputation. He humbled Himself (Phil. 2:7-8). The One who shared God's glory with Him before the world began was laid as a babe in a manger (John 17:5; Luke 2:7). Ultimately, He traded a crown of glory for a crown of thorns.

The old hymn asks, "Why did my Savior come to earth and to the humble go? Why did He choose a lowly birth?" And the answer echoes back, "Because He loved me so!" For the love of unlovable sinners Jesus left His heavenly home to come into a world of sin. He bid farewell to those "ivory palaces" and to the Father who had loved Him from all eternity. "Only His great eternal love, made my Savior go."

And His Father did not merely *let* Him go. He sent Him. Jesus would not have come had it not pleased the Father to send Him (John 8:29). So God also "showed his love for us when he sent his only Son into the world to give us life" (1 John 4:9, CEV).

## MISSION IMPOSSIBLE – MADE POSSIBLE!

From a human standpoint, Jesus was sent from heaven on an impossible mission. In order to make His Father's home our home too, He would need to become human, live a perfectly sinless life, sacrifice Himself for unworthy humanity, come back to life from the grave, and then return to heaven to pave the way for men. It strains the mind to even imagine how such things could be accomplished. But, "Is anything too hard for God?" (Genesis 18:14). "The things which are impossible with men are possible with God" (Luke 18:27).

We live in an age when many things once thought humanly impossible have now been accomplished, from running the four-minute mile, to men walking on the moon, to the election of a black U.S. president. But none of these compare even to the first step of Jesus' impossible mission. How could God's Son come to earth? How does God become man? Impossible! Can't be done! Yet God's power and wisdom would accomplish it.

The Lord had long ago declared that He would do the impossible. "The virgin shall conceive and bear a Son, and shall call His name Immanuel" (Isa. 7:14). Nonetheless, the young virgin Mary was stunned when the angel Gabriel appeared to her announcing that she would conceive and bear the Son of God. "How can this be?" she asks. The angel responds, "The power of the Highest will overshadow you" (Luke 1:34-35). It took the power of the Highest to do it: "But when the fullness of the time had come, God sent forth His Son, born of a woman…that we might receive the adoption as sons" (Gal. 4:4-5).

How does a man live the sinless life necessary for Him to become the perfect sacrifice? Again, some would say it is impossible! It had certainly never been done! Sin was the undefeated heavyweight champion of the world. Every man who had ever lived had been knocked to his knees by its brutal force. But Jesus comes "in the likeness of sinful flesh" and pounds Sin to the canvas (Rom. 8:3). He takes every blow of temptation thrown by Sin, but never wavers, never falters, never falls. He "was in all points tempted as we are, yet without sin" (Heb. 4:15). The bout was long and hard, a grueling contest of strength and will, and Christ "suffered, being tempted," but He "committed no sin" (Heb. 2:18; 1 Pet. 2:22). He emerges as the victor, the spotless lamb, the sinless sacrifice, the Captain of our salvation perfected through suffering (1 Pet. 1:19-20; Heb. 2:10).

How does a man conquer death? Magician and famous escape artist Harry Houdini tried it. Before his death, he worked out a code with his wife Bess so that he might contact her from the afterlife. This would be his greatest escape! After Houdini's death on October 31, 1926, Bess held annual séances to get in touch with Harry. She conducted a séance every year for ten years, but she never heard from him. Eventually she stopped trying, explaining that "ten years is long enough to wait for any man." The greatest escape artist in human history could not escape the clutches of death. But Jesus did.

The perfectly sinless Son of God was killed on a cross. He was beaten, abused, and then crucified. A Roman soldier thrust a spear into His side to confirm that He was truly dead (John 19:34). He was. His friends and loved ones had watched his final moments, and a crowd of onlookers had mourned His passing (Luke 23:48-49). He was gone. There could be no doubt. His lifeless, mangled body was laid in a new tomb hewn out of rock, and a large stone was rolled against the door of the tomb (Mark 15:46). A detachment of guards was set at the tomb, and the tomb was securely sealed (Matt. 27:66). Escape would have been impossible for any mere man. Ask Houdini.

But death had met its match this time. The tables were turned. Now the impossible thing was for death to hold its prey. God raised up His Son "having loosed the pains of death, because it was not possible that He should be held by it" (Acts 2:24). The impregnable gates of Hades, the realm of the dead, were unlocked and thrown wide open by the mighty power of God.

Those black gates could not prevail to hold the Christ or prevent His kingdom from being established (Matt. 16:18). God's Son came forth and declared, "I am He who lives, and was dead, and behold, I am alive forevermore. And I have the keys of Hades and of Death" (Rev. 1:18). He came out of the grave and opened the gates of Hades so wide that others who had been held there strolled out with Him. Like hopeless prisoners long held in the darkest of dungeons, what a thrill it must have been for them to welcome One into their midst who carried the keys to the prison! Their "graves were opened; and many bodies of the saints who had fallen asleep were raised; and coming out of the graves after His resurrection, they went into the holy city and appeared to many" (Matt. 27:52-53). He who conquered sin had conquered death.

Three days after His crucifixion, there was no body in His tomb. There still isn't. In Jesus' day, the Jews could visit the tomb of their forefather David who died and was buried centuries before, but seven weeks after the crucifixion of Christ they could not produce the body of Jesus (Acts 2:29). It has been observed that the pyramids of Egypt are famous because they contain the mummified bodies of ancient Egyptian kings. Westminster Abbey is noted because it holds the remains of many English nobles and notables. Arlington National Cemetery in Washington, D. C. is revered because it is the resting place of many outstanding Americans whose names are known and inscribed there on stones, and for a soldier whose name is unknown. But the tomb of Jesus is famous because it is empty. It stands as a testament of hope.

As we ponder that empty tomb and Him whose resurrection it declares, we are compelled to proclaim with the apostle Peter, "Blessed *be* the God and Father of our Lord Jesus Christ, who according to His abundant mercy has begotten us again to a living hope through the resurrection of Jesus Christ from the dead to an inheritance incorruptible and undefiled and that does not fade away, reserved in heaven for you" (1 Pet. 1:3-4). Here rests your hope and mine. The *impossible dream* of a heavenly home for sinful man suddenly enters the realm of *real possibility* and becomes *a living hope* through the resurrection of Jesus Christ.

But Jesus' mission is not complete at His resurrection. There is one final long step to be taken.

## THERE AND BACK AGAIN – MISSION ACCOMPLISHED!

On July 21, 1969, Neil Armstrong stepped out of the Apollo Lunar Module onto the surface of the moon and declared, "That's one small step for a man, one giant leap for mankind." A giant leap for mankind indeed! The culmination of so much planning, work, and human ingenuity enabled Armstrong to take that incredible step for all of us. Although there are doubters who proclaim it was all a hoax, most of us accept the moon landing as reality. We are certain that a man went to the moon. And if one man went, others could follow.

The ascension of Jesus back to heaven after His resurrection is an event of monumental significance, yet it is seldom studied or contemplated as being important in its own right. It is the final step in Jesus' long journey from heaven, to earth and back home again. It explains where Christ is now, how He got there, and why His followers can expect to go there too. As Jesus told His disciples, "if I go and prepare a place for you, I will come again and receive you to Myself, that where I am, there you may be also" (John 14:3). Later, as their eyes beheld Him levitating to the realm beyond, angels assured these disciples that "This *same* Jesus, who was taken up from you into heaven, will so come in like manner as you saw Him go into heaven" (Acts 1:11).

Jesus' own teaching reveals the importance of His ascension. In John chapter six, Jesus declares Himself to be the bread of life which *came down from heaven* (6:51). He explains that anyone who wishes to live forever must eat this heaven-sent bread; they must take Him into their souls, rely on Him for sustenance, and allow Him to abide within them and become part of them. Many

who heard Jesus on that occasion *could not swallow* His claim that
He had come down from heaven. They said, "This is a hard
saying; who can understand it?" Jesus asked them, "What then if
you should see the Son of Man ascend where He was before?"
(John 6:62).

It is one thing to claim to come down from heaven, but it is
quite another to ascend back there. Only Jesus completed that
round trip. "No one has ascended to heaven but He who came
down from heaven, that is, the Son of Man who is in heaven"
(John 3:13).

As Jesus completes His mission, He returns to His Father's
home and sits down at His side (Eph. 1:20). The Old Testament
priests could never sit down because their work was never done.
The sacrifices they offered could never take away sins. Under the
Law of Moses, "every priest *stands* ministering daily and offering
repeatedly the same sacrifices, which can never take away sins."
In contrast, Jesus, "after He had offered one sacrifice for sins
forever, *sat down* at the right hand of God" (Heb. 10:11-12). At
the completion of His long impossible mission, Jesus gets to sit
down at last. The "finisher of our faith" returned home and "sat
down at the right hand of the throne of God" (Heb. 12:2).

## OUR LADDER UP TO HEAVEN

The Book of Hebrews calls upon us as "partakers of the
heavenly calling" to "consider the Apostle and High Priest of our
confession, Christ Jesus" (3:1). As children of God, we have been
called by heaven to heaven; it is crucial that we have fully in our
view the One who was sent to earth to make us God's children, and
Who returned to heaven to lead us to our home.

Jesus is our apostle in that He is the One whom God "has sent
forth" from heaven to earth that we might become God's children
(Gal. 4:4-5). The phrase "has sent forth" is translated from the
Greek verb *ex apostello* which has an obvious connection to the
noun apostle (Gr. *apostolos)*. Jesus is our High Priest in that He
has opened the way for us that we might follow Him into the
presence of God. He is our forerunner, going before us into the
presence of God, blazing a bright trail so that we might have a
clear path.

Long ago, the patriarch Jacob dreamed a dream in which a ladder was set up on earth that reached to heaven. He saw angels ascending and descending on that ladder. The meaning was that God would bless Jacob and His descendants, continually sending help from heaven to minister to their needs.

Hundreds of years later, Jesus Christ Himself declares that He is such a ladder. "You shall see heaven open, and the angels of God ascending and descending upon the Son of Man" (John 1:51). Jesus stretched Himself from heaven to earth to bless mankind and to give us a way to get to God. He is the anchor chain of hope from our souls to the Presence of God Himself (Heb. 6:19).

*As to the pilgrim patriarch that wondrous dream was given,*
*So seems my Savior's love to me, a ladder up to heaven.*[1]

Heaven is indeed like a dream. But it is a dream that can come true because of Jesus. He made the impossible possible. He blazed the trail, brightened the way, and bids us follow Him...home.

---

[1] Elizabeth C. Clephane, "Beneath the Cross of Jesus" as quoted in John Phillips, *The View from Mount Calvary*, Kregel Publications, 2006.

## QUESTIONS

1. Describe the relationship that Jesus had shared with His Father in heaven before the world began. (John 17:5, 24; Phil. 2:7-8)


2. What are some of the factors that motivated Jesus to leave heaven to come to earth? (John 8:29; Phil. 2:4-8; 1 John 4:9; Gal. 4:4-5)


3. After Jesus left heaven to come to earth, what were the things He needed to accomplish before returning to heaven to be with His Father?


4. What is the significance of Jesus' ascension back to the Father? How does this event relate to our hope of heaven?


5. In what sense are we "partakers of the heavenly calling"? (Heb. 3:1)

*Chapter Three*

# "What is Man that You are Mindful of Him?"

A nerdy-looking computer geek marries a supermodel, and the world gawks in amazement. What does she see in him? How could she care about him? Is this some kind of joke? Perhaps David was wondering something similar, but on a much grander scale, when he asked God this question: "What is man, that You are mindful of Him, and the son of man that You visit him?" (Ps. 8:4).

God cares about us. He thinks about us. In fact, His thoughts about us "are more than can be numbered" (Ps. 40:5). He "visits" us with salvation (Ps. 106:4). But what could God possibly see in *man?* Why would He stoop so low as to save us and bring us home to His eternal abode? He is so high and powerful, and we are so lowly and weak, that the magnitude of His condescension astounds us.

When I was a boy, my family lived for several years in Colorado Springs, Colorado. Our house faced Pikes Peak, and we needed only to look out the picture pane window of our living room to behold its grandeur. At 14,114 feet above sea level, Pikes Peak is the farthest east of the big peaks of the Colorado Rockies. It intrudes onto the plains. Our house, which was about 20 miles from the summit, sat at less than 6,000 feet above sea level. The vertical drop from peak to plain is over 8,000 feet, or about a mile and a half. But that is nothing compared to the distance God spans when He stoops down from His lofty throne and the rarefied air of heaven to visit man.

As the Psalmist David seeks to help us comprehend this wonder, he mingles together a consideration of two grand truths. The first is that God possesses unimaginable majesty, power and wisdom as evidenced by the physical creation. And the second is that it is this awesome God who Himself placed man in such a significant position within His creation – a little lower than the angels, but having dominion over the work of God's hands. Our status in creation was ordained by God Almighty as part of His eternal plan.

## "WHEN I CONSIDER YOUR HEAVENS..."

The eighth Psalm is sometimes called "The Astronomer's Psalm." It begins and ends with this declaration: "O LORD, our Lord, How excellent is Your name in all the earth." There is nothing on earth greater or more majestic than the name of the Lord. And there is scarcely anything that demonstrates His greatness more than the heavens, the moon and the stars which He ordained. Truly, "The heavens declare the glory of God; and the firmament shows His handiwork" (Ps. 19:1).

But even with this great cosmic demonstration of God's divine power, can we fully comprehend it? Not according to Job. In awestruck wonder he observes that God "hangs the earth on nothing. He binds up the water in His thick clouds, yet the clouds are not broken under it...by His Spirit He adorned the heavens... Indeed these are the mere edges of His ways, and how small a whisper we hear of Him! But the thunder of His power who can understand?" (Job 26:7-8, 13-14). In the majesty of creation, we perceive only the *mere edges* of God's ways. We hear just a *whisper* of His greatness. We have no concept of the full thunder of His majestic power. How wondrously loud and overwhelming it must be! "God thunders marvelously with His voice; He does great things, and we do not understand." (Job 37:5).

Perhaps a few observations about the size of the universe, found in a simple children's book, may help us grasp how immense our world is, and how great is the One who formed it. In a book entitled *Is a Blue Whale the Biggest Thing There Is?*, Robert Wells takes us from a size we can easily grasp to one that is mind boggling. He explains that the largest animal on earth is the blue whale. Just the flippers on its tail are bigger than most animals on earth. But a blue whale isn't anywhere near as big as a mountain. If you put one hundred blue whales in a huge jar, you could put millions of whale jars inside a hollowed-out Mount Everest. But Mount Everest isn't anywhere near as big as the earth. If you stacked one hundred Mount Everests on top of one another, it would be just a whisker on the face of the earth. And the earth isn't anywhere near as big as the sun. You could fit one million earths inside of the sun. But the sun, which is a medium-size star, isn't anywhere near as big as the red supergiant star called Antares. It is estimated that fifty million of our suns could fit inside of Antares. But Antares isn't anywhere near as big as the Milky Way galaxy. Billions of stars, as well as countless comets and asteroids, make up the Milky Way galaxy. But the Milky Way galaxy isn't anywhere near as big as the universe. There are billions of other galaxies in the universe. And yet, filled with billions of galaxies, the universe is almost totally empty. The distances from one galaxy to another are beyond our imagination.

The Creator of this universe is God. He is bigger than all of it! He spoke it all into being (Heb. 11:3). He upholds it all with his mighty power (Heb. 1:3). Great is our God and greatly to be praised! "Let all the earth fear the LORD; Let all the inhabitants of the world stand in awe of Him. For He spoke, and it was done; He commanded, and it stood fast" (Ps. 33:8-9).

## "YOU HAVE MADE HIM A LITTLE LOWER THAN THE ANGELS"

It is this great God who positioned man in his place in creation. And it is *because* we stand in awe of our Creator's power and wisdom that we must accept our place with unquestioning humility and grace. "Will the thing formed say to him who formed it, 'Why have you made me like this'?" (Rom. 9:20).

The mention of man's position relative to the angels is of far reaching significance. The New Testament writers quote this fact to demonstrate both the humiliation and exaltation of Christ. He "was made a little lower than the angels for the suffering of death"

(Heb. 2:9). And then, "when He had by Himself purged our sins, He sat down at the right hand of the Majesty on high, having become so much better than the angels, as He has by inheritance obtained a more excellent name than they" (Heb. 1:3-4). In being made a little lower than the angels in order to die as a man for our sins, Jesus descended far beneath His true position. However, when He had purged our sins, He ascended back to His rightful place beside His heavenly Father, *so much better than the angels.*

But our main point now is to consider what it means for all men to be positioned by God "a little lower than the angels." Angels are "greater in power and might" than we are (2 Pet. 2:11). They are "mighty" (2 Thess. 1:7). Yet, like us, they were created to serve the Lord and glorify Him. The Psalmist writes, "Bless the LORD, you His angels, who excel in strength, who do His word, heeding the voice of His word. Bless the LORD, all you His hosts, you ministers of His, who do His pleasure" (Ps. 103:20-21; cf. 148:2-5).

The incredible thing is that these amazing spiritual beings have been directed by God to minister on our behalf. Hebrews 1:14 indicates that angels are "all ministering spirits sent forth to minister for those who will inherit salvation." That God would create such glorious beings and assign them to work for the benefit of men speaks volumes about God's love for us and the special place we hold in His creation.

Concerning God's compassion for His children in ancient times, Isaiah 63:9 states, "In all their affliction He was afflicted, and the Angel of His Presence saved them; In His love and in His pity He redeemed them; and He bore them and carried them all the days of old."

God's love for men can be traced through the Old Testament through the activity of angels. God sent His angel to comfort the outcast Hagar and the downcast Elijah (Gen. 16; 1 Kings 19). An angel appeared to Moses in the burning bush and directed Him to deliver the Israelites from bondage (Acts 7:35). The Law of Moses was appointed through angels (Acts 7:53; Gal. 3:19). God directed an angel to guide the Israelites in the wilderness and lead them to the Promised Land (Exod. 23:20-23). Later, it was an angel who stirred Gideon to be used by God to bring deliverance to Israel, and it was an angel who shut the lions' mouths to protect Daniel (Judg.

6; Dan. 6:22). In each of these Bible examples, and many more that could be cited, we see angels being used by God on man's behalf – the high and holy serving the weak and lowly.

The New Testament also contains numerous accounts of the activity of angels. They appear frequently in the life of Christ. Early on we see them at the annunciation to Mary (Luke 1:26) and the proclamation of His birth to shepherds in a field (Luke 2:9); later, angels minister to Jesus after His temptation and as He prayed in the Garden (Matt. 4:11; Luke 22:43). Angels were also used in the New Testament to give special direction, information, or encouragement to evangelists. Philip, Peter, and Paul all received help or instruction from angels (Acts 8:26; 12:6-11; 27:23). John was shown the visions of Revelation by angels (Rev. 21:9-10; 22:8).

Angels are still concerned with us today. They desire to look into our salvation (1 Pet. 1:12), and "there is joy in the presence of the angels of God over one sinner who repents" (Luke 15:10). Ultimately it is the angels who gather the lost and "cast them into the furnace of fire" (Matt. 13:41-42), and who collect the souls of the saved and carry them to blissful rest (Luke 16:22). And on the last day, when the Lord returns to resurrect and judge all men, the angels will be with Him, ushering the saved to life eternal, where we shall ever be with the Lord (1 Thess. 4:16-17; 2 Thess. 1:7-10). In a later chapter, we will discuss the help God sends from heaven to aid us on our journey to our eternal home, but let us say here and now that one of the greatest of those gracious helps comes in the form of God's holy angels.

As important as they are in the story of man's redemption, it is nonetheless noteworthy that angels were never assigned the task of directly saving man or even of telling a lost man what to do to be saved. An angel appeared to unsaved Cornelius and told him to send for Peter who would tell him "words by which you...will be saved" (Acts 10:3-6; 11:13). An angel told Philip to go to a place where he would meet an Ethiopian in search of salvation (Acts 8:26). The saving power of the gospel was given to men to share with men; the lost hear, believe and call on the Lord for salvation as a result of preachers preaching the gospel (Rom. 10:13-15).

## YOU HAVE MADE HIM TO HAVE DOMINION OVER THE WORKS OF YOUR HANDS

In Genesis 1:26 God said, "Let Us make man in Our image, according to Our likeness; let them have dominion over the fish of the sea, over the birds of the air, and over the cattle, over all the earth and over every creeping thing that creeps on the earth." Here, no doubt, is what David has in mind when he declares that the Lord made man "to have dominion over the works of Your hands" and has "put all things under his feet" (Ps. 8:6).

Most of us have a sense that there is something special about the life of a human. To illustrate, imagine that you are driving down the road, and the brakes go out on your vehicle. You cannot stop. You are on a downhill grade. As you round a curve, there is an old lady standing in the middle of the road who has gone out to bring in her dog, which is now standing on the left side of the road; to the right there is a parked car which you immediately recognize as a late model Mercedes. You can't stop your car; you can only steer it. Which way will you steer? Will you choose to hit the woman, the dog or the Mercedes? Each has its value. But even in our age of animal rights and materialism, most of us would prefer to hit the dog or the car before we would hit the woman. Why? Is it not because we somehow understand that the woman is far more valuable?

Jesus knew our worth. He said, "Look at the birds of the air; they do not sow or reap or store away in barns, and yet your heavenly Father feeds them. Are you not much more valuable than they?" (Matt. 6:26). Indeed, we are more valuable, for we have been made in the image of God. Any *person* is more valuable than any *thing*.

Our likeness to the image of God is not in our physical form, but rather it is in our spiritual nature. God is a Spirit (John 4:24). He is an eternal Spirit who has put both "spirit" and "eternity" into the hearts of men (Eccl. 3:11; Job 32:8). As C.S. Lewis said, "There are no ordinary people. You have never talked to a mere mortal." We relate to God on a spiritual level, spirit to Spirit. Unlike any other being in the physical creation, we can perceive beauty, righteousness, grace, holiness and eternity. We are capable of having a sentient relationship with God. A major part of Paul's argument to the Athenians in Acts 17 is that God put us on this earth so that we might come to know Him and understand His nature (Acts 17:26-30). And this ability of men to know God, an ability that is unique among all the creatures of earth, is what makes eternal life possible for us. Jesus prayed to the Father in the presence of His disciples and said, "This is eternal life, that they may know You, the only true God, and Jesus Christ whom You have sent" (John 17:3).

So what is man? He is but a creature, but he is a creature created with a soul in the image of his Maker. And from His home in heaven, our Maker sent His Son to bring us to His eternal home that we might see His face and commune with Him forever and ever. These facts are the inception of our hope. These are the foundational truths which enable us to begin to dream for a home with God.

Faith is the victory that overcomes the world.

Eccl 3:

Elohim = Magesties

Zakariah 13:6

Lord's supper- constant reminder

QUESTIONS

*Isaiah*
*55:8,9*

*Isaiah 64:8*   *Jeremiah 18:*

1. How does God's sovereignty and superiority over man help us accept our place in His creation?
*Psalm 8: (Because he loves us, but we are so miniscule.) Pg. 26 last para.*

2. Although angels are greater in power and position than men, God has assigned them the task of ministering to us. What does this indicate concerning God's estimate of human worth? *Heb 1:14*

3. Give examples from both Old and New Testaments illustrating how angels have been used by God to benefit mankind. *Ex.   Daniel     Gen—Cherubim*
*Gen 6:*
*Gal 3:18,19    Acts & Acts 12:*

4. What present and future activity of angels shows that they have concern for our eternal well-being?

5. Why are there no examples in Scripture of angels appearing to humans to tell them what to do to be saved? What is the God-ordained process for getting the gospel message to the lost? *Person to person   saved to Lost*
*Lk 16.*

6. What makes human life more valuable than animal life? In what way or ways are humans significantly different from every other creature on earth? *Gen 2:7  No man*

7. How does the answer to the question "What is man?" relate to our hope of heaven? *Pg 26*

*Jerimiah*

*Chapter Four*

# $J$esus $P$repares $U$s $F$or $T$he $M$oment

It's called the "Miracle on Ice." Well, actually it *wasn't* a miracle, but it *was* nothing short of remarkable.

We're talking about the 1980 Winter Olympics when some college players from the USA brought down the greatest hockey team in the world, the mighty Red Machine from the USSR! It was a victory that roused a slumbering nation and ignited once again a patriotism quelled by the negativism of the 70's. Americans needed something to dream about.

Sport's Illustrated said of it, "It may just be the single most indelible moment in all of U.S. sports history." The closing seconds are etched in our minds as broadcaster, Al Michaels, calls the action: *"Eleven seconds. You got ten seconds, the countdown going on right now. Five seconds left in the game! Do you believe in miracles? Yes!"* What a moment!

This was no fluke. Much of the success of this team is credited to its coach Herb Brooks. "The romantic notion that a bunch of college scrubs felled the world's greatest team through sheer pluck and determination is misguided. Brooks spent a year-and-a-half nurturing the team. He held numerous tryout camps, which included psychological testing, before selecting a roster from several hundred prospects. He challenged them physically, but also verbally, questioning whether they were good enough, tough enough, worthy of the task" (Miracle on Ice: American Hockey's Defining Moment, Jamie Fitzpatrick, About.com). Player Mike Ramsey said, "He messed with our minds at every opportunity."

In his now famous pre-game speech, Brooks began, *"Great moments are born from great opportunity and that's what you have here tonight boys."*

For the faithful children of God the greatest of all moments is coming! The greatest of all speeches will be delivered after victory is ours! Our King and Savior will say to us on that day:

> *"Well done, good and faithful servant;*
> *you were faithful over a few things,*
> *I will make you ruler over many things.*
> *Enter into the joy of your lord."*
> (Matt. 25:21)

Here then is the **great moment** we have the **great opportunity** to achieve. This is what we have here boys and girls. But it doesn't come to us without effort and submission to our Leader.

You may be wondering why this book does not immediately jump to the joys of heaven, showing its splendor and describing what it is like there. Hang on...we get there. But just as a hockey team does not immediately make it to the dream, neither do the people of God. Heaven must be prepared for. This is what Jesus came to do; to prepare us. This is what takes so much time. Even Jesus spent precious little time describing the beauty of heaven while here on earth. He spent more hours stressing that we must *"strive to enter"* (Luke 13:23-24). Forget about trying to count how many go there. Just make sure *you* enter!

Without our Leader's training, we are a bunch of misfits, ill-prepared for heaven. But making "silk purses out of sow's ears" is the Lord's business.

## GET YOUR HEAD IN THE GAME

Jesus doesn't "mess with our minds" in the same way Brooks did with his hockey team. But He certainly does drill it into us that we must have disciplined minds that will not be deterred from laying hold of heaven.

The late baseball great, Yogi Berra, who got quite a reputation for his hilarious one-liners, once said, "Baseball is 90% mental. The other half is physical." Ole Yogi might not have always put the words together right, but he was "spot on" in stressing the mental discipline needed on the road to victory. The journey to heaven is the same.

This is why Peter wrote in his first epistle, *"Gird up the loins of your mind"* (1 Pet. 1:13). It's why Paul wrote, *"Be transformed by the renewing of your mind"* (Rom. 12:1-2). Paul's own tenacity in pursuing heaven is perhaps best spoken in Philippians 3 where he passionately says:

"Not that I have already attained, or am already perfected;
but I press on, *that I may lay hold of that*
*for which Jesus has laid hold of me.*
Brethren I do not count myself to have apprehended;
but *one thing I do,*
forgetting those things which are behind
and *reaching forward* to those things which are ahead.
*I press toward the prize of the upward call of God in Christ Jesus."*
(Phil. 3:12-14)

Are we surprised that the next words are, *"Let us, as many as are mature, have this mind"* (Phil. 3:15)? Jesus is not looking for superstars. He is the only Star in this thing. He is looking for people, even though scrubs, who are willing to center their minds on the one thing that matters. They surrender to Him in order to let Him shape their character to fit heaven. They will let nothing stop their pursuit of "the moment." To arrive there, a specific *road to glory* must be traveled.

HIGHWAY TO HEAVEN

Before Jesus came to earth, extensive efforts began to construct the highway which would lead to heaven: a spiritual *road to the gold.* All of us are familiar with the work men do when they build highways. They fill in ravines, blast away mountains, and work to make a crooked way, straight.

In a spiritual sense, this was the work of John the Baptist, the forerunner to Jesus. He came to begin construction on the road that would first *bring Jesus to us* and then *lead us to Him.* The heavy duty work is done on our hearts and minds; for indeed, our sin has made our hearts crooked. The signs would read, "Minds Under Construction."

Listen to how Isaiah describes the work of John the Baptist upon the hearts of men.

> *"The voice of one crying in the wilderness:*
> *'Prepare the way of the Lord,*
> *make His paths straight.*
> *Every valley shall be filled*
> *and every mountain and hill brought low;*
> *and the crooked places shall be made straight*
> *and the rough ways made smooth;*
> *and all flesh shall see the salvation of God.'"*
> (Luke 3:4-6)

I personally believe that the coming of God to earth was so extraordinary that men would never have been ready for it without the paving work of the prophets and men like John the Baptist. It was shocking enough even with advance notice! God coming to earth doesn't happen every day, you know! Thus, God saw fit to send a forerunner. So much preparatory work had to be done. It reminds me of the extensive prep work that is done long before the President of the United States visits a city. And boy, do people ever snap into shape cleaning the place up! Or maybe it compares to what happens among slackers on a job when someone says, "The boss is coming!"

Well, in essence that's what John did. He began to cry out because God was about to be with us (Matt. 1:23)!

## REPENT: THE FIRST WORD OF THE GOSPEL

John the Baptist came on the scene like a bulldozer or a powder man blasting away with powerful words.

> *"Repent, for the kingdom of heaven is at hand!"*
> (Matt. 3:2)

31

Here was the call for us to change. He barked out commands for *a change of mind, resulting in a change of direction.* It was a call to leave the road of sin and darkness for the road of light. We must understand that we **will not** make it to heaven without changing, without repenting. Repentance is the first word of the gospel...a truth first made clear to me by Richard Owen Roberts.

First words are often crucial, indispensable words designed to get our immediate attention. It's like crying out to a child who is about to run out in front of an oncoming car. With urgency we shout, "**STOP!!** A car is coming!" We want the child to hear the first word above all. STOP!! If we did it in reverse order and took the time to say, "A car is coming. STOP!," it might be too late. Understand?

When Jesus arrived, it was among the first words from His lips too.

> *"From that time, Jesus began to say,*
> *'Repent for the kingdom of heaven is at hand.'"*
> (Matt. 4:17)

After He had ascended to heaven, His ambassador Peter was asked by sinners on the day of Pentecost, *"Men and brethren, what shall we do?"* Peter's first word was...repent!

> *"Repent and let every one of you*
> *be baptized in the name of Jesus Christ*
> *for the remission of sins and*
> *you shall receive the gift of the Holy Spirit."*
> (Acts 2:38)

This too was what Jesus told all of the apostles to teach. It was the first word on their lips (Mark 6:12; Luke 24:47). And when Paul was chosen by the Lord to preach to the Gentiles, Jesus told him to preach that they should repent and turn to God (Acts 26:19-20). Are we getting it?

**Change and preparation.** Without it, a hockey team does not travel a road to glory. Without it, a President will not make his way to our city and walk among us. And without it, *we* never start on the highway that leads to heaven.

## "THE KINGDOM OF HEAVEN IS LIKE UNTO..."

In His three-and-a-half short years of ministry, Jesus spent His time teaching about a coming kingdom that would last forever, while all earthly kingdoms were going to fall. As we sing, *"The kingdoms of earth pass away one by one but the kingdom of heaven remains. It is built on a rock and the Lord is its King. And forever and ever He reigns."* We can enter this kingdom by becoming Christians. We have a foretaste of it here. But at the last, our joy climaxes, when we enter the everlasting glories of heaven.

> *"for so an entrance will be supplied*
> *to you abundantly into the*
> *everlasting kingdom of our Lord*
> *and Savior Jesus Christ."*
> (2 Pet. 1:11)

My use of the USA hockey team to introduce this chapter reveals my great love for my earthly country. But the USA is like every other kingdom (nation). The day will come when it, like all the others, will fade away. Only the kingdom of heaven will remain, and in it we will see many from various nations who surrendered their lives to its KING (Rev. 21:24; Dan. 2:44). The words of Jim Elliot are riveting here. *"He is no fool who gives up what he cannot keep, to gain that which he cannot lose."*

To get us ready for that day, Jesus often says words like, *"The kingdom of heaven is like unto..."* and then moves into an earthly parallel we can understand. He loved clothing truth with story. Jesus was always simple, yet profound. This explains why so many of the common people heard him gladly. Simple truths were reaching humble hearts hungry for things eternal.

For example, Jesus taught that this kingdom is so valuable, **it is worth everything we may give up to obtain it**. I love His words.

> *"Again the kingdom of heaven*
> *is like a treasure hidden in a field,*
> *which a man found and hid;*
> *and for joy over it he goes and*

33

> *sells all that he has and*
> *buys that field."*
> (Matt. 13:44)

> *"Again, the kingdom of heaven is like*
> *a merchant seeking beautiful pearls,*
> *who, when he had found one pearl of great price,*
> *went and sold all that he had and bought it."*
> (Matt. 13:45)

Jesus is doing all He can to get us to see that NOTHING compares to the value of this kingdom and we must be willing to give everything for it. And my friend, that means giving *yourself* also. The King will take second place to no one.

> *"If anyone comes to Me and*
> *does not hate his father and mother,*
> *wife and children, brothers and sisters,*
> *yes, and his own life also,*
> *he cannot be My disciple."*

> *"So, likewise, whoever does not forsake*
> *all that he has cannot be my disciple."*
> (Luke 14:26,33)

Is this plain enough? Now, don't misunderstand Jesus. He is not saying for us to hate our family members, but He is stressing that the intensity of our love for them or for ourselves cannot touch the degree of our love for Him. He takes first place...ALWAYS! We must not forfeit the kingdom of heaven for anyone (Matt. 10:37).

## *THEIRS* IS THE KINGDOM OF HEAVEN

Jesus' most well-known treatise on the kingdom of heaven is His sermon on the mount, masterfully taught and recorded in Matthew 5-7. It must be read and absorbed. We might think of it as the *constitution of the kingdom*. In three short chapters, Jesus helps us to see much of what it will take to travel this narrow road that leads to eternal life (Matt. 7:13-14).

In the opening words of the sermon (the beatitudes), Jesus reveals the character *every* kingdom citizen strives to possess. Twice before He finishes these kingdom qualities, He says *"for* **theirs** *is the kingdom of heaven"* (Matt. 5:3,10). It's for a certain kind of person.

Now, let's get personal with this. Are you going to be this kind of person? Will you see the incomparable value of the kingdom? Will you be willing to make whatever sacrifices are necessary to enter it? Will you, with God's help, develop the holiness that heaven's citizens must develop? People who do not love holy living *here* will never enjoy it *there*. God is not going to snap His fingers and make you love heaven later.

C.S. Lewis, once an agnostic himself, argues that not everyone would enjoy heaven. In his words, *"The grass hurts their feet"* (The Great Divorce). He means that some people are so entrenched in ungodly living that they would not enjoy the holiness of heaven. They are uncomfortable. J.C. Ryle writes, *"Without holiness on earth we shall never be prepared to enjoy heaven. Heaven is a holy place. The Lord of heaven is a holy Being. The angels are holy creatures. Holiness is written on everything in heaven...How shall we ever be at home and happy in heaven if we die unholy? Death works no change. The grave makes no alteration. Each will rise again with the same character in which he breathed his last. What will be our place if we are strangers to holiness now?"* (Holiness, J.C. Ryle, pg. 28).

I am persuaded he is right! Do you love doing spiritual things now? Will you, with great pleasure, pursue heavenly things? If you are determined to do so, you can make the cut. The Lord will only take such people on His dream team.

## QUESTIONS

1.  What are the wonderful words of Matthew 25:21, and how do you think it will make you feel to hear those words spoken to you on the day of judgment? Will everyone hear those words? Explain.

2.  How important is it to have our minds focused and disciplined as we live here below and prepare to go to heaven? Elaborate.

3.  Why was the work of John the Baptist so important?

4.  What did this chapter emphasize is the first word of the gospel? Give examples of it being the first word on the mouths of God's messengers?

5.  What does it mean to repent, and why is repentance a matter of first importance?

6.  In what ways did Jesus emphasize the unsurpassed value of the kingdom of heaven?

7.  Do you agree with the thought that some people would not enjoy heaven? Why or why not?

8.  What do you see expressed in the words, "theirs is the kingdom of heaven"?

*Chapter Five*

# "Unless One Is Born Again"

We turn our attention now to the greatest of all questions, **"What Must I Do To Be Saved?"** Taking our sins away was not God's ultimate aim. Some seem to think so. Too many rise from the waters of baptism, check it off their list of "things to do" and then move merrily along with the rest of the world. God's aim has always been to have a people who can live with Him forever. Removing our sins is simply getting rid of *the problem* so that He can then begin to make us what we ought to be. Creating us anew is what the Bible calls the "new birth." Jesus could not have been more emphatic about us having to be changed. Again, without change, we will not go to heaven. Listen to Him.

> **"Most assuredly, I say to you, unless one is born again, he cannot see the kingdom of God."** (John 3:3)

You see, heaven is a pure place with no defilements. In that city, graffiti will never be splattered throughout what was once a pretty place. It will forever be majestic because no one is allowed to disturb it. Peter reminds us that it is *"an inheritance incorruptible and undefiled, and that does not fade away, reserved in heaven for you"* (1 Pet. 1:3). John writes, *"But there shall by no means enter in, anything that defiles, or causes an abomination or a lie, but only those who are written in the Lamb's book of Life"* (Rev. 21:27). The people who go there will add to its beauty for they too are beautiful pieces of work created by God, His unique workmanship (Eph. 2:10). They are saved, recreated, and in character look identical to its original inhabitants for they have taken on the nature of the divine family (2 Pet. 1:4).

Salvation is a beautiful process – it is God's work. Without His plan of salvation there would have been nothing we could do to reverse our hopelessness (Rom. 5:6-8). Let's look at God's wonderful plan, the process Jesus called being "born again."

## THE CROSS: THE GROUND OF OUR SALVATION.

If we take the cross of Christ away everything else comes crumbling down. Without His death and resurrection everything else is in vain. *"And if Christ is not risen, your faith is futile; you are still in your sins"* (1 Cor. 15:17)! Without the shedding of His blood there is no remission of sin (Heb. 9:22; Matt. 26:28). The cross then is our only boast (Gal. 6:14).

I love the story of an elephant that was crossing an old bridge. A mouse asked for a ride and happily positioned himself on the back of the elephant. As the monstrous behemoth stomped on across, the bridge groaned and creaked under the strain. When they made it to the other side, the mouse triumphantly proclaimed, "We sure shook that thing; didn't we big boy!" How absurd for that little creature to think he added anything to that accomplishment. And neither have we. When it comes to saving our souls, God has done the shaking! And ironically, when Jesus died, heaven and earth shook (Matt. 27:51; Heb. 12:26).

Our sins separated us from God. We were a great distance apart. It was as though God stood on one side of a great chasm and we stood on the other with no way for us to bridge that gap. We had no power to save ourselves solely by our effort. What did God do? In essence, He laid the cross of Jesus across the chasm and invites us to be reconciled to Him: to walk Calvary's bridge back to Him. This is the message of Romans 5:6-11, where Paul proclaims, *"For when we were still without strength, in due time Christ died for the ungodly"* (Rom. 5:6). The bad news is this: if we refuse to be reconciled to God, we cannot be saved from His wrath.

## HEARING AND BELIEVING THE MESSAGE OF THE CROSS

Having laid forth the ground of our salvation, God next moves to preach the good news to all who will listen. It is called "the message of the cross" (1 Cor. 1:18). It is essential to the new birth. Unless we know we are sick, we will never come to the Great Physician for the cure.

The sacrifice of Jesus is enough to break into the hardest of hearts. All one has to do is read the book of Acts and see what its message did to its first converts. In Acts 2, when those Jews realized that Jesus was their Messiah who had died for them, the wording was *"they were **cut to the heart**"* (Acts 2:37). **They believed.** Can you imagine the feelings that shot through them when they realized the long awaited Messiah had been killed...by them? They believed!

Seeing their sins and the cost to the Son of God, they desired to change their lives and asked, *"Men and brethren, what shall we do?"* (vs. 37). This is God's aim in preaching the cross. He wants all to come, but their coming is by no means guaranteed. A few chapters later, others who heard the same message were also ***"cut to the heart,"*** but they killed Stephen, the one who preached it to them (Acts 7:54,58).

Are we seeing how important the preaching of the cross is in being born again? But the process of the new birth goes further.

## TURNING TO GOD: REPENTANCE

As mentioned earlier, the first word from Peter's mouth to those who asked, "What must we do" was... **"repent"** (Acts 2:38).

With God's word implanted as seed in the heart of the believer (James 1:21), a desire is produced to undergo a radical change of heart and life. Perhaps it is best seen in the life of Saul of Tarsus who previously tried to kill Christians and then after his conversion amazingly was trying to convert as many as he could to Christ. Now, that's repentance! It was such an astounding turn that Paul's fellow Jews said, *"Is this not he who destroyed those who called on this name in Jerusalem?"* (Acts 9:21). He is a man preaching *"the faith which he once tried to destroy"* (Gal. 1:23). They could hardly believe what they were seeing and hearing from him.  He was a different man.

A change just as radical must be ours.  *"Repent therefore and be converted that your sins may be blotted out, so that times of refreshing may come from the presence of the Lord"* (Acts 3:19).

OLD MAN BURIED, NEW MAN RISES: BAPTISM

Having changed our minds and deciding to turn to God, the person in the process of being born again by the Spirit of God is ready to bury the old man of sin and be raised a new man.  He *dies* in order to *live*.  This happens beautifully as he surrenders to God in baptism.  The convicting work of the Spirit, through the preached message, has brought him to this watery grave.

> *"Unless one is born again*
> *of the **water** and the **Spirit**,*
> *he cannot enter the kingdom of God."*
> (John 3:5)

In baptism, the gospel message is re-enacted.  Romans 6 shows the reenactment.  The gospel message is that **Jesus died by crucifixion, Jesus was buried, and Jesus was raised to a new, unending life**.  This form or pattern is laid out in Romans 6, and **we trace it precisely** to be delivered from our sins.   Can you see the parallels?

| | |
|---|---|
| *Jesus was crucified.* | *We crucify our old man (Rom. 6:6).* |
| *Jesus was buried.* | *We bury the old man of sin in baptism (Rom. 6:4).* |
| *Jesus was raised.* | *We are raised to a new life (Rom. 6:4).* |

In baptism we are saying "good riddance" to our old man.  We have taken up our cross, laid ourselves upon it, and ended our old life!  In Jesus' day, you might see a man walk by with his cross, but you never saw him come back.  The cross finished him.  It ended his old pattern.  The cross had its way.  So it must be with us. We determine at this moment that the old ways are over and the cross will have its way with us.

This truth is illustrated well in a baptism I once heard of. A man called Jerry was being baptized and his brother went along to witness. When they arrived at the river, the water was turbulent. As Jerry entered the rapid water, his brother cried out, *"Jerry, don't do this. A man could die doing this."* Jerry shouted back, *"Precisely! It has taken me years to figure that out."*

The purpose of baptism is clearly stated in the Bible. It is *"for the remission of sins"* (Acts 2:38), to *"wash away sins"* (Acts 22:16), and to *"save us"* (1 Pet. 3:21). God performs this wonderful work with His hands as He washes us in the blood of Christ (Rev. 1:5). It is *His operation*, not ours (Col. 2:11-13). To our joy, as we go through life, God gives us **a precise moment to reference and know that we were saved**. Having obeyed the form, we never have to roam about with insecurities about whether we were ever saved. In baptism, we called upon God to cleanse us and wipe our consciences clean, and He did as He had promised!

The conversion of the Ethiopian eunuch highlights the process of being born again. Take time to read about it in Acts 8:26-39.

- He heard the gospel message about Jesus' life and Jesus' death (vs. 35).

- He saw water and asked *"What hinders me from being baptized?"* (vs. 36).

- He confessed with his mouth that Jesus Christ was the Son of God (vs. 37).

- He was buried in baptism (Acts 8:38).

- He arose from the watery grave to a new life and went on rejoicing (vs. 39).

Long time gospel preacher Bill Hall tells of teaching a woman the Lord's plan of salvation and using the conversion of the Ethiopian eunuch. As he finished, she said, "I see all of that, but it still looks to me like a person has to be born again." Bill replied, "Well, maybe we just saw what is involved in being born again."

Of course the eunuch was born again. He was convicted by the Spirit (born of Spirit). He repented. He confessed His faith in the Lord who died for him. He was baptized (born of water) and renewed by the same Spirit. He was added to the kingdom (Col. 1:13). This is the new birth.

Once our old sins are washed away, we have not arrived. As previously said, taking our sins away was not God's ultimate aim. It only removed the problem. Sure, we can be counted by Him as holy in *position* (in Christ). What God wants is for us to be holy in *practice* (1 John 3:4-9). With my sins newly washed away, I am **just like Jesus in position** – pure and unblemished. Now, God wants me by practice to **become like Jesus in all my thoughts and actions**. This will take great focus and diligence, and the new child of God should be excited and ready to get with the program! We may be on the team, but now we go for the gold!

## PRESSING TOWARD THE GOAL

The Lord's team is made up of people who truly want to become like Jesus. This is the essence of Christianity: being like Him, perfectly trained. They let their coach work with them to transform them. They understand that it will take great diligence on their part: the straining of every ligament.

The apostle Paul likely had Olympics in mind when he wrote Philippians 3. Three important principles are seen in the following:

**First, we see his willingness to give up all to follow Christ**. Paul was a practicing Jew and a persecutor of Jesus. But in a lightning fast moment of time, he realized just how wrong he was when Jesus appeared to him on the road to Damascus! His entire life changed after that. I can only imagine what all went through his head for the three days he was without sight, refusing to eat and drink, and spending his time in prayer. He later became a Christian and gave up all he could have achieved in Judaism.

With no hesitation he says, *"But indeed I count all things loss for the excellence of the knowledge of Christ Jesus my Lord, for whom I have suffered the loss of all things, and count them as rubbish, that I may gain Christ"* (Phil. 3:8). His past life was considered rubbish – a word for "table scraps" or "dung on a field." Pretty graphic! The word "loss" is the same word used of people who throw everything overboard in a sea storm. It may be costly to toss, but it's not worth losing your life (Acts 27:9,18-19). What will you and I have to toss? Count the cost!

**Next, we see His pursuit to gain Jesus and heaven.** His great desire was to be in Christ and be counted righteous by the Lord's sacrifice and forgiveness (Phil. 3:9). This he could never have if he remained in the religion of his youth (Acts 13:38-39). He wanted to know Jesus intimately and become like Him even through suffering (Phil. 3:10).

**At the last, we see a determination to let nothing stop him from crossing the finish line.** He surely had the mindset of an athlete. He never allowed himself to get an inflated ego thinking he had arrived. He kept pressing for more. He knew Jesus laid hold of him for a reason, and he intended to see what was at the end of the journey! He kept reaching forward to the things ahead. He said, *"I press toward the goal for the prize of the upward call of God in Christ Jesus"* (Phil. 3:14).

This great servant of the Lord says determination must be the mindset of us all if we are to ever stand on the eternal stage to receive our medals from the Lord. Notice the emphasis in the passage.

"Nevertheless, to the degree that
we have already attained,
let us walk by the ***same rule***,
let us be of the ***same mind***.
Brethren, join in ***following my example***,
and ***note those who so walk***,
as you have us for ***a pattern***."
(Phil. 3:16)

Paul used the same athletic imagery in 1 Corinthians 9:24-27, where he compares our desire for heaven to running a race and to boxing. It is not a race where we have to beat everyone else across the finish line. To *finish* is to *win*. But we do run it as if only one

43

can win. We must be so driven. We strive for mastery. We exercise self-discipline and self-control. True athletes do not give in to things that slow them down. We are well-aimed, not beating the air but hitting the mark. And the person we have to beat upon the most is ourselves. We guard ourselves carefully so as not to be disqualified.

While writing this chapter, I paused for a moment and let my mind slip into a little daydream. I pictured the great judgment day. Judgment had concluded, and in my mind I saw all the saved being ushered toward the eternal city and imagined what it would be like if I was left behind. I thought of the wonderful things they were soon to enjoy. Soon they would be seeing God and seeing Jesus, standing in the presence of the Holy Spirit, seeing the angels, seeing the men and women read about in the Bible, and seeing the splendor of heaven. Honestly, my mind recoiled. I simply could not stand the thought of missing out on that great moment! May God help me and help you, dear reader, to embrace the dream and let our Leader train us to that end. Heaven will surely be worth it all!!

## QUESTIONS

1. What word in John 3:3 shows that we absolutely cannot go to heaven without being born again?

2. **Thought question:** What would it do to heaven if sinners made no changes yet still went to heaven?

3. Why is the cross the ground of our salvation? Strive to answer thoroughly.

4. What did Christ do for us when we had no strength (power) to save ourselves?

5. List all the things involved in being born again.

6. How do we trace or duplicate the gospel when we are baptized?

7. What is the purpose of baptism according to the Bible? Use several verses. Who is working for us in baptism?

8. Clearly, the Ethiopian eunuch was born again (Acts 8:26-39). What things do we see involved in his conversion?

9. Once we have been made holy in *position*, what does God want us to do all throughout our life as a Christian?

10. Look at Philippians 3. What mindset must we have to press toward the goal of heaven?

## Chapter Six

# "Conformed to the Image of His Son"

Imagine that you are handed a new invention – something you have never seen before. You don't know what it is. You don't know its purpose. How could you find out? It can't tell you! It is possible that you could find out through trial and error or guesswork, but the wisest thing to do would probably be to ask its inventor. The intended function of any invention is best understood by its creator.

Have you ever pondered your existence? Why are you here? Why did God create you? What's life all about? What's the meaning of it all? In His word, God gives a pretty simple answer to these questions. We must go there to get His answer! God knows why He made us, and He knows our purpose!

## GOD'S ETERNAL INTENTION

God said that "He chose us in Him before the foundation of the world, that we should be holy and without blame before Him in love, having **predestined us to adoption as sons** by Jesus Christ to Himself, according to the good pleasure of His will" (Eph. 1:4-5). Simply put, we are here to become God's children!

It has been observed that the size of a family is often determined by the demeanor of the first child. If the firstborn is fussy or difficult as an infant, and then grows to become disobedient and insufferable as a toddler, mom and dad may decide they don't want any more children! But when that first child's disposition is sweet, and parenting is joyous and fulfilling, the family may well get pretty big.

Our heavenly Father had the perfect Son from all eternity. He wants more children *just like* that perfect One. In Romans 8:29, the Scripture says that "whom He foreknew, He also predestined to be **conformed to the image of His Son** that He might be the firstborn among many brethren." God's intention is not just to have a lot of children, but to have a lot of children who are like His first child.

## A FAMILY RESEMBLANCE

I am told that on a wall near the main entrance to the Alamo in San Antonio, Texas, there is a portrait with the following inscription:

> *James Butler Bonham—no picture of him exists.*
> *This portrait is of his nephew, Major James Bonham, deceased,*
> *who greatly resembled his uncle.*
> *It is placed here by the family that people may know the*
> *appearance of the man who died for freedom.*

No literal portrait of Jesus exists either. But His likeness lives in those who have been born again according to the will of God. In becoming children of God, we put on the very likeness of Christ: "For you are all sons of God through faith in Christ Jesus. For as many of you as were baptized into Christ have put on Christ" (Gal. 3:26-27).

One of our first inclinations when we see a newborn baby is to look for physical features resembling parents, grandparents, or other relatives. "She has her mother's eyes!" we exclaim. Or, "That nose is just like his daddy's." While our observations usually have some basis in fact, the reality is that a newborn looks more like other newborns than any adult member of the family. But as the child grows and matures, we may begin to see true likenesses, not only in physical form, but also in personality and temperament.

A newborn child of God is not yet all that God has begotten him to be. He has put on Christ, but he has some growing to do before he is a complete Christ-like man and has reached any true "measure of the stature of the fullness of Christ" (Eph. 4:13).

The apostle Paul was concerned that as the Christians in Galatia grew, they did not resemble Christ. He addresses them as, "My little children, for whom I labor in birth again until Christ is formed in you" (Gal. 4:19). Their lack of Christ-likeness was painfully evident. They held on to Moses' Law instead of faith in Christ (5:4-6). They were biting and devouring one another (5:15). And they seemed to have had trouble accepting Paul's repeated warnings that those who practice the works of the flesh cannot inherit the kingdom of God (5:19-21). If they had truly "put on the Lord Jesus Christ" they would "make no provision for the flesh, to fulfill its lusts" (cf. Rom. 13:14).

Metaphorically, Paul was going through labor pains once again in his efforts to make the Galatians recognizable as children of God. As yet, some of them bore little resemblance to Christ. Paul's desire is that Christ be "formed in" them. The word *formed* in Galatians 4:19 is translated from a Greek word from which we get the English word *morphed*. To borrow some terminology from the old children's television show *Power Rangers*, it was *morphing time* for the Galatians. The very form of their inner man needed to be changed. The essence of Paul's plea to the Galatians is, *"Give Christ your heart; make heaven your goal! Let Jesus dwell within your soul" (Vernie Prichard)*. In a manner of speaking, the DNA of Christ would alter their souls at the cellular level, and the change would be evident in their lives.

Paul's hope was that his own example would serve as a model for the Galatians and for us. He declares, "I have been crucified with Christ; it is no longer I who live, but Christ lives in me" (Gal. 2:20). He wanted the hearts of the Galatians to resound with the self-same sentiment, one that we ourselves may have expressed in the words of an old hymn: *"Oh! to be like Thee, blessed Redeemer, This is my constant longing and prayer; Gladly I'll forfeit all of earth's treasures, Jesus, Thy perfect likeness to wear!" (Thomas O. Chisholm)*.

## CONFORMING BY COPYING

Most of us have had role models and heroes in our lives. They are people that we want to try to be like. One of the most emulated sports figures in modern times is Michael Jordan. With six NBA titles, five MVPs, ten scoring titles, and fourteen All-Star appearances, Michael Jordan's legacy on the basketball court is astounding. At the height of his professional basketball career, few faces in America were more recognizable than his. An advertising campaign by Nike encouraged us all to "Be Like Mike!" and many athletes and wanna-be athletes tried to do just that. When Jordan shot a free throw with his eyes closed, kids on playgrounds all across America had to try it too. They watched him closely on television. They were glued to the nightly highlight reels of his games. They listened to the post-game interviews. And, they copied his moves, his shot, and even the way he held his tongue. When it came to playing basketball, millions wanted to be like Mike!

You may never have wanted to be like Michael Jordan, but wouldn't it be something if you could be like Christ Jesus, the only begotten Son of God! The marvelous implication of being *born again* is that you can be. For as surely as we have borne the image of Adam, the man of dust, "we shall also bear the image of the heavenly man," Jesus Christ (1 Cor. 15:49).

As Christians, we "have put on the new man who is renewed in knowledge according to the image of Him who created him" (Col. 3:10). Notice that to put on the image of Christ, we must be "renewed in knowledge." We cannot be like Him if we don't know what He looks like! If we want to be like Christ, we must give our closest attention to His every deed and every word. We will watch the inspired highlight reels of His life recorded in the gospels of Matthew, Mark, Luke and John. We will practice to be like Him. And then we will go out in the world, and purposely imitate His every move…even to the way He held His tongue (cf. Isa. 53:7).

How many people in this world claim to be Christians who have never bothered to inform themselves *from Scripture* concerning how Jesus lived, what He taught, and what He expects of His followers? We must focus on learning Him! If we want to

49

grow to be like Him, we must grow in our knowledge of Him (2 Pet. 3:18). "A disciple is not above his teacher, but everyone who is perfectly trained will be like his teacher" (Luke 6:40).

By constantly visualizing the Christ we are shown in Scripture, we come to know Him and become like Him. It is as if we are looking into a magic mirror. "We all, with unveiled face, beholding as in a mirror the glory of the Lord, are being transformed into the same image from glory to glory..." (2 Cor. 3:18). The word *transformed* here refers to a metamorphosis. It literally means, "to change into another form" (cf. Matt.17:2; Rom.12:2). To be *conformed* to the image of God's Son, we must be *transformed* from what we are to what we see in Him.

It has been said that imitation is the sincerest form of *flattery*; it does a pretty good job of passing for *praise* as well. Imitating another declares our admiration.

Ephesians 5:1 teaches us to become "imitators" or *mimics* of God "as dear children." Many parents have discovered to their own embarrassment what great mimics their children are. Children imitate parents and older siblings in word and in deed. They seldom misquote. In fact, they usually repeat word for word everything you shouldn't have said. Those who are striving to become sons of God will engage in this same kind of unabashed, continual mimicry. The only difference is that, in imitating our Father and our Older Brother, we will never have cause to say or do anything that we shouldn't.

## TRANSFORMATION THROUGH TRIAL

Christ is our perfect example. He suffered even though He never said or did anything wrong. He left us an example that we should follow in His steps (1 Pet. 2:21). Our road to becoming Christ-like will involve suffering as well. The cross is the instrument of death for our earthly man, but also the tool of our transformation that we must bear to become like the Heavenly Man.

As the One who transforms us into sons of God, and leads us to our heavenly home, Christ suffered. Hebrews 2:10 states that "It was fitting for Him, for whom are all things and by whom are all things, in bringing **many sons** to glory, to make the Captain of their salvation **perfect through sufferings**." "Therefore, since Christ suffered for us in the flesh, arm yourselves also with the same mind" (1 Pet. 4:1).

No normal person *wants* to suffer. But since Christ suffered, we are willing to suffer that we may be like Him. Jesus said, "If anyone desires to come after Me, let him deny himself, and take up his cross daily, and follow Me" (Luke 9:23). Our Christ-like cross is the *daily* burden of duty and of suffering.

> *"I took up my cross to follow the Lord,*
> *and I followed Him for a day.*
> *At the next day's dawn the Lord had moved on,*
> *and I did not know the way.*
> *The cross I had borne at yesterday's morn*
> *seemed longingly to say,*
> *"To go after Him, you must bear me again,*
> *and again, and again, each day."*

As Thomas à Kempis wrote in *The Imitation of Christ*, "Jesus has now many lovers of the heavenly kingdom but few bearers of His cross." Satan tries to deceive us into thinking that children of God should not have to suffer. Nothing could be further from the truth. If we are children of God, we are striving to be like His only begotten Son in every way. We are never more Christ-like than when we are suffering for righteousness' sake. No one can fully know Christ or imitate Him until he knows "the fellowship of His sufferings" (Phil. 3:10). It is the cost of discipleship.

## ACTUALITY OR ACTING?

As children, we all learned to act or play roles. When I was little, we'd pretend to be Superman or Batman, or soldiers, or cowboys and Indians. But I never actually was a superhero, or a soldier or a cowboy or an Indian. I was just acting.

In our spiritual lives, acting is not good. The English word *hypocrite* is from the Greek word *hypocrite*; it's one of those words in the English Bible where the translators seem to have gotten a little lazy and just brought a Greek word over into English. If it were actually translated instead of transliterated, it would probably have been rendered *actor*. Like stage actors in a Greek play, the huge masks that hypocrites wear conceal their true identities; they are not who they appear to be. Jesus said that hypocrites "are like whitewashed tombs which indeed appear beautiful outwardly, but inside are full of dead men's bones" (Matt. 23:27).

The Bible teaches us to lay aside all "hypocrisy...as newborn babes desire the pure milk of the word that you may grow thereby" (1 Pet. 2:1). Our first *duty* as newly born children of God is to stop acting! We're not pretending to be good; we are becoming good! One of the first impulses of a newborn is to desire nourishment! Like an infant craving milk, we constantly desire God's word, not because we are forced to, but because we need it to live and to grow so that we might become what we were born to be.

Hypocrites just won't go to heaven (Matt. 24:51). Heaven is not a masquerade; it's more like a come-as-you-are banquet, but the only ones who are admitted entrance are those who have truly engaged themselves in the process of becoming Christ-like. Therefore, our sincere goal here in this life is to strive to be like Him.

## THE ETERNAL MAKEOVER

The transformation God planned for us is not completed in this life. The apostle John writes, "Beloved, now we are children of God; and it has not yet been revealed what we shall be, but we know that when He is revealed, we shall be like Him, for we shall see Him as He is" (1 John 3:2). While it has not been revealed precisely what we will be, we will be like Christ in having bodies that are incorruptible, immortal, heavenly, spiritual and glorious (1 Cor. 15:47-59). But the key point is that we will be *like Christ,* having been completely conformed to the image of God's Son. "As we have borne the image of the man of dust, we shall also bear the image of the heavenly Man" (1 Cor. 15:49). Jesus said that "those who are counted worthy to attain that age, and the resurrection from the dead...are sons of God, being sons of the resurrection" (Luke 20:35-36).

There is a yearning in every child of God for the moment of that final transformation. "For our citizenship is in heaven, from which we also eagerly wait for the Savior, the Lord Jesus Christ, who will transform our lowly body that it may be conformed to His glorious body..." (Phil. 3:20-21). All of our hopes and dreams, our strivings and aspirations, will be realized at last. And we will look upon the face of our Redeemer, and see Him as He is, and be like Him.

Miley Cyrus sang, *"Ain't about how fast I get there. Ain't about what's waiting on the other side. It's the climb."* But, the truth is that it is about what is waiting on the other side! What is waiting is Immanuel's land, and you will be a son of God. Your Heavenly Father is there to receive you – the One who created you to become His own child.

The transformation we are undergoing now is but a prelude to our final eternal transformation. For when we reach the end of time, it is not the end of our existence, but the beginning of our true existence. C.S. Lewis wrote the following words about his fictional characters as they came to the end of their world in *The Chronicles of Narnia:*

*"For us this is the end of all the stories...but for them it was only the beginning of the real story. All their life in this world had only been the cover and the title page; now at last they were beginning Chapter One of the Great Story, which no one on earth has read, which goes on forever and in which every chapter is better than the one before."*

And in that great eternal story, we will finally and at last bear the image of the Heavenly Man and stand among ***many brethren*** who have been conformed to the image of God's Son for all eternity.

## QUESTIONS

1. What is the answer to the question, "Why are we here?" What is God's eternal intention for man? (Eph. 1:4-5; Rom. 8:29)

2. What had the Galatians done to "put on Christ"? (Gal.3:27)

   - In what ways were they still un-Christ-like? (Gal. 5:4-21)

   - For what was Paul laboring as if in birth pains? (Gal. 4:19)

   - How would this process take place?

3. What must we know in order to conform to Christ by copying Him, and how can we attain such knowledge?

4. Why would anyone desire to participate in the sufferings of Christ?

5. Explain the difference between a hypocrite and a child who imitates his parents.

6. Why isn't heaven like a masquerade or a costume party?

7. What are some of the ways we will be like Christ in heaven?

## Chapter Seven

# *Living a Heavenly Life on Earth*

**Have you noticed** how we tend to dilute the meaning of words by overuse? Words like *epic* and *awesome* are constantly used to describe things that are neither truly epic nor awesome – everything from ballgames, to ice cream, to what's for lunch. These words have been so incessantly and subtly misapplied that most of us no longer know their original meanings.

It reminds me of a classic line from the movie, *The Princess Bride*. In the movie, a pompous character named Vizzini repeatedly uses the word *inconceivable* to describe events which he believed could not happen, but which were in fact happening. Finally, his companion, Inigo Montoya, says to him, "You keep using that word. I do not think it means what you think it means!"

In the English speaking world, people keep using words like *heavenly* to describe things that are anything but *heavenly*, and words like *hell* to describe experiences which bear no valid resemblance to *hell*. How many times have you heard someone declare that they have "been through hell"? The Scriptures teach that hell is a place of unparalleled anguish and misery – a place of darkness, weeping, and gnashing of teeth, where the worm does not die and the fire is not quenched (Matt. 25:30; Mk. 9:43-48). No one could ever actually "go through" hell because there is no getting out of it; it is "everlasting punishment" (Matt. 25:46).

The concept of heaven has been subjected to usages that are similarly profane. How often have you heard the word *heavenly* being used to refer to earthly things which bear no resemblance to heaven at all? Surely, no one really believes that there are handbags, hams, and hairdos that can accurately be described as *heavenly*.

We say all this to make the point that, in this chapter, we are not using the word *heavenly* in any diluted, profane, or accommodative sense whatsoever. To be sure, the life that the child of God lives on earth is not the life that he will live in heaven, but it is a life that is infused with heavenly realities and relationships. It is a life that is directed by heaven, gives its allegiance to heaven, is in fellowship with heavenly beings, and is lived to glorify the Father who is in heaven.

## HEEDING HEAVENLY WORDS – THE MESSAGE FROM OUT OF THIS WORLD

Living a heavenly life begins when a person heeds the heavenly message. Jesus came directly from heaven to communicate God's nature and God's will to mankind. Jesus is the very Word of God who has declared God to man (John 1:18). In His conversation with Nicodemus in John chapter three, Jesus explains that men can only testify to what they have seen or experienced. Therefore, as the Son of Man, Jesus could speak "heavenly things" because He alone among men had witnessed them. "No one has ascended to heaven but He who came down from heaven, that is, the Son of Man who is in heaven" (John 3:13).

From heaven, God has "spoken to us by His Son" (Heb. 1:2). And because the words of Jesus are heavenly in their origin, they also carry the authority of heaven. Jesus said, "For I have not spoken on My own authority; but the Father who sent Me gave Me a command, what I should say and what I should speak" (John 12:49).

But Jesus did not reveal the entirety of the heavenly message during His earthly ministry. Even His closest followers could not have handled it (John 16:12). Before Jesus ascended back to heaven, He told His apostles that He would send to them the Holy Spirit who would guide them into *all truth* from heaven:

> *"However, when He, the Spirit of truth, has come, He will guide you into all truth; for He will not speak on His own*

> *authority, but whatever He hears He will speak; and He*
> *will tell you things to come. He will glorify Me, for He will*
> *take of what is Mine and declare it to you. All things that*
> *the Father has are Mine. Therefore I said that He will take*
> *of Mine and declare it to you."*
> *(John 16:13-15)*

Later, after the apostles had been filled with the promised Holy Spirit as recorded in Acts the second chapter, they too would speak words directly from heaven. In 1 Peter 1:12, the apostle Peter declares that the message of salvation has "been reported to you through those who have preached the gospel to you by the Holy Spirit sent from heaven." The apostle Paul affirms that the things he spoke were "words…which the Holy Spirit teaches," and that "the things that I write unto you are the commandments of the Lord" (1 Cor. 2:13; 14:37).

So, the message of Jesus and of His Spirit-inspired apostles and prophets is a heavenly message. Those who love Jesus will heed it, and the Father and the Son will come to them and make their home (John 14:23). Talk about a heavenly life! The words and deeds of those who live such a life are directed and authorized by heaven (cf. Col. 3:17). Their destiny is heaven.

In contrast, those who refuse to hear and heed the heavenly message are in a precarious position. They are living earthly lives. They have rejected the authority of the Father in heaven. And like many who have rebelled against Him in times past, their destiny is destruction. Be cautioned that this is a fate that we ourselves shall "not escape if we turn away from Him who speaks from heaven" (Heb. 12:25). "Therefore we must give the more earnest heed to the things we have heard, lest we drift away" (Heb. 2:1).

Careful and constant attention to the heavenly message is foundational for living a heavenly life on earth.

## IN CONTACT WITH HEAVEN

Millions of dollars and untold man hours have been invested by humans in an effort to communicate with extraterrestrial beings. The world's largest radio telescope, measuring 1,000 feet across and located at the Arecibo Observatory in Puerto Rico, has been used to send messages into outer space in an attempt to make contact with intelligent life. As of yet, there is no indication that any such message has been received. But apparently a lot of people, some of whom refuse to believe in the God of heaven, would like to talk to someone in the heavens.

None who have lived life on earth have been so attuned to heaven as Jesus Christ. It must not escape our notice that the One who brought God's word *from* heaven also regularly communicated *to* heaven while He walked as a mortal man. According to Scripture, Jesus prayed many times in the presence of others (e.g. Luke 3:21; 22:17-19; John 6:11; 17:1-26); He also "would often go to some place where He could be alone and pray" (Luke 5:16, CEV).

The most heavenly life that was ever lived was lived by One who was in constant communication with heaven. Those of us who long for a heavenly life on earth would do well to emulate Jesus in this and every way. He is the One whom the Scriptures describe as "the heavenly Man." And, "as *is* the heavenly *Man,* so also *are* those *who are* heavenly" (1 Cor. 15:48).

Jesus' role as our High Priest makes it possible for us to communicate with heaven as He did. For Christ has entered "into heaven itself, now to appear in the presence of God for us." (Heb. 9:24). Jesus lives to make intercession for us (Heb. 7:25), enabling the words of our prayers to be heard in the throne room of our Heavenly Father. In the beautiful word pictures of the Book of Revelation, the incense that rises from the altar before the very throne of God is identified as "the prayers of the saints" (Rev. 5:8; 8:3-4). The sweet aroma of our prayers is ever in the presence of God.

With such free access, there is no reason for any child of God to be out of touch with heaven. We may confidently and continually contact the realm above. "Seeing then that we have a great High Priest who has passed through the heavens, Jesus the Son of God...Let us therefore come boldly to the throne of grace, that we may obtain mercy and find grace to help in time of need" (Heb. 4:14, 16). Let us continue "steadfastly in prayer" (Rom 12:12).

## HEAVENLY CITIZENSHIP

The realm in which God the Father reigns is known in Scripture as "the kingdom of heaven." In God's book, this precise phrase is found only in the gospel of Matthew where it occurs thirty-two times.

Among the important truths we may learn about the kingdom of heaven in Matthew's gospel include the fact that it was "at hand" or imminent in Jesus' day (Matt. 3:2; 4:17; 10:7). The establishment of the kingdom would not linger for thousands of years, as some have supposed. In Matthew 16:18-19, Jesus promises to build His church and then immediately tells the apostle Peter that He would give him "the keys of the kingdom of heaven." Peter used "the keys" to open the door into the church or kingdom when he preached on the day of Pentecost in Acts 2, and about 3,000 people believed, repented, and were baptized into Christ for the remission of their sins (Acts 2:38-41, 48). The clear implication is that all those who enter the church, enter the kingdom of heaven.

These truths coincide with other facts we learn in Matthew's gospel concerning those who would become citizens of the kingdom of heaven. To enter the kingdom of heaven, one must *repent* and be *converted* (Matt. 3:2; 4:17; 18:3). Significantly, Jesus taught that it would take more than merely acknowledging Him as Lord to be part of the kingdom; entrance into the kingdom would only be granted to one who "does the will of my Father in heaven" (Matt. 7:21). Citizens of the kingdom of heaven would further be characterized by *righteousness* which exceeded that of the scribes and Pharisees and by *humility* like that of a little child (Matt. 5:3, 10, 20; 18:3).

For Christians today, as Paul joyfully proclaims in Philippians 3:20, "our citizenship is in heaven." We are in this world but not of this world, for we "have come to Mount Zion and to the city of the living God, the heavenly Jerusalem, to an innumerable company of angels, to the general assembly and church of the firstborn who are registered in heaven, to God the Judge of all, to the spirits of just men made perfect" (Heb. 12:22-23). Those in the church have their names enrolled as citizens of heaven. They are depicted as dwelling in the city of the living God and being surrounded by its glories. Whatever difficulties we may have in understanding the depths of what is being described in this text, it is clear beyond question that the inspired writer wishes to impress upon us the heavenly nature of that to which we have come as Christians. Commenting on this passage, Albert Barnes wrote the following:

> *"It is true that Christians have not yet seen that city by the physical eye, but they look to it with the eye of faith. It is revealed to them; they are permitted by anticipation to contemplate its glories, and to feel that it is to be their eternal home. They are permitted to live and act as if they saw the glorious God whose dwelling is there, and were already surrounded by the angels and the redeemed. The apostle does not represent them as if they were expecting that it would be visibly set up on the earth, but as being now actually dwellers in that city, and bound to live and act as if they were amidst its splendors."*

## HEAVENLY FELLOWSHIP

My ancestors, and probably yours, immigrated to the United States where they were thrilled to become citizens. In so doing, they entered into a relationship with every other American citizen. There is a common bond between all of us. Despite differences in social status, education, racial or cultural backgrounds, we are all Americans, and ideally that means that we share a love and devotion for our country and a mutual desire for its success. As one, we cheer our Olympic athletes and mourn our national tragedies. We chant "U-S-A" in unison for any sports team that represents our country, and we sing "God Bless America" with one voice in the aftermath of madmen flying airplanes into the Pentagon and World Trade Center. Even our money proclaims the idealism of our unity, engraved as it is with the Latin phrase "E Pluribus Unum" which means "Out of Many, One."

As Christians, when we enter the kingdom of heaven, "we are no longer strangers and foreigners, but fellow citizens with the saints" (Eph. 2:19). Notice the phrase "fellow citizens." The relationship we share transcends earthly bounds, for God has "raised us up together, and made us sit together in the heavenly places in Christ Jesus" (Eph. 2:6). Our common bond is more than just an allegiance to heaven; it is experiencing together a life that is heavenly. We are sitting *together* in heavenly places. And Christ is with us in this realm. For, "truly our fellowship is with the Father and with His Son Jesus Christ" (1 John 1:3).

This wonderful fellowship is contingent on walking in the light. Those who accompany each other on the same path will share the same journey and thus arrive at the same destination. The path to heaven is a pathway of light! Some who walk in darkness may claim to be in fellowship with heaven and try to pretend as if they are enjoying it, but they are deceiving themselves and others. "If we say that we have fellowship with Him, and walk in darkness, we lie and do not practice the truth. But if we walk in the light as He is in the light, we have fellowship with one another, and the blood of Jesus Christ His Son cleanses us from all sin" (1 John 1:6-7).

## WORSHIP — BREATHING THE AIR OF HEAVEN

In Revelation chapters 4 and 5, the apostle John is given a glimpse into the throne room of God. He hears the praise given to the One who sits on the throne: "You are worthy, O Lord, to receive glory and honor and power; for You created all things, and by Your will they exist and were created" (Rev. 4:11). John sees "every creature which is in heaven and on the earth and under the earth and such as are in the sea, and all that are in them," and he hears them saying, "Blessing and honor and glory and power be to Him who sits on the throne, and to the Lamb, forever and ever!" (Rev. 5:13).

While we live on earth, our proximity to heaven may never be nearer than when we are engaged in worship. Through praising our God, we live in His presence. "Surely the righteous will praise your name, and the upright will live in your presence" (Ps. 140:13, NIV). Those who cannot see the importance of taking the time to worship God on earth would certainly feel out of place in heaven.

The psalmist David, whose life was filled to overflowing with worship, saw himself as alive in God's house. Despite the earthly tribulations he experienced in his early adult years, he wrote, "I am like a green olive tree in the house of God; I trust in the mercy of God forever and ever. I will praise You forever…and in the presence of Your saints I will wait on Your name…" (Ps. 52:8-9).

To illustrate how worship sustains our spiritual lives while we walk this earth, Craig Brian Larson reminds us of an amazing incident that occurred in October of 1988:

> *The world watched as three gray whales, icebound off Point Barrow, Alaska, floated battered and bloody, gasping for breath at a hole in the ice. [The whales, which had been discovered by a native hunter, had injured themselves by ramming their heads into the ice in order to breathe and keep the small opening from freezing over – sk]. Their only hope: somehow to be transported five miles past the ice pack to open sea. Rescuers began cutting a string of breathing holes about 20 yards apart in the six-inch-thick ice. For eight days they coaxed the whales from one hole to the next, mile after mile. Along the way, one of the trio vanished and was presumed dead; but finally, with the help of Russian icebreakers, the whales Putu and Siku swam to freedom.*
> *In a way, worship is a string of breathing holes*
> *the Lord provides for His people.*[2]

Although we may be wounded and exhausted in a world frozen over with evil, with no oxygen for the soul, we rise together for air in worship. We breathe, as it were, the air of heaven itself as we adore and glorify our heavenly Father. In this way, our struggling souls survive the journey through this cold world, until that day when the barrier between us and heaven melts away at last, and we inhale deeply and freely, that we may exhale in voices of eternal praise.

Heaven is truly the culmination of a journey to our eternal home. And, as we have seen, the journey itself is so enveloped with heavenly things that when those who have traveled the path together finally enter the heavenly city, the surroundings will not seem strange or foreign at all. It will just feel like home.

*Psalm 22:3 But thou art holy, O thou that inhabit the praise of Israel*

*Be on the Alert!*
*Stand Strong in the faith!*

QUESTIONS   ~Surprise as joy~ - CS Lewis

*In these last days He has spoken to us through his Son.*

1. In what form or forms has the message from heaven come to earth?

Jn 16:12-15 Guide the Apostles into all truth. 1 Pet

Jn 1:8 living word incarnate   Heb 1:1,2,3

Jesus is the very word of God. Jesus came down from Heaven — Jn 3:13, Jn 12:49

2. What are the consequences if we turn away from Him who speaks from heaven? Eternal Death. Heb 12:25 Be lost. Heb 2:1 Heed the warning. Do not drift away

3. How did Jesus Christ, the One who came from heaven, keep in contact with heaven when He walked on earth?
Prayer. Luke 3:21, Jn 6:11  17:1-21
Luke 5:16
Jesus - the Heavenly Man" "Son of man 1 Cor 15:48-49

4. How does Jesus enable us to keep in contact with heaven today? Prayer Luke 3:21, Jn 6:11  17:1-21
Luke 5:16 + Heb 7:25  1 Tim 2:5
Enables our prayers a sweet incense Rev 5:8, 8:3-4

Heb 4:14,16 We have a greathigh priest

5. According to the Gospel of Matthew, what are some of the key characteristics of those who gain citizenship in the kingdom of heaven? Kingdom of heaven is mentioned 32 times in Mt. The Realm in which God the Father reigns. In Jesus day it was imminent not 32, 4:17, 10:7 one must be converted & repent 3:2 4:17, 18:3

6. How do we maintain fellowship with other heavenly citizens while on earth? (Eph. 2:19; 1 John 1:3-7)

7. Is there a sense in which our worship here on earth is like breathing the air of heaven itself? How so?
Miracle - 3 whales

8. What are the key components to living a heavenly life on earth? Prayer - worship - fellowship, faith
(We recieve not, because we ask not) Col 3

Heb 12:22-28   Rev 4:1

1 Jn 1:6-7 The path to heaven is a heaven of light

*Chapter Eight*

# Working to be Rewarded and Remembered

**As I write these words,** the Christmas season is upon us in North Alabama. Stores are jammed with parents buying gifts for children, many of whom have been told that they had better be good if they expect to receive the presents they've asked for. The kids are dreaming about getting their presents, and parents are scurrying from place to place in an all-out effort to find those special gifts. No one blames parents for using those highly prized gifts to reward and encourage better behavior from their children. Most of us understand and appreciate this concept. So does our Heavenly Father.

## HEAVEN AS A REWARD

The definition of a *reward* is "something desirable given in return for what somebody has done" or "a benefit obtained as a result of an action taken or a job done" *(Encarta)*. The Greek word most often translated *reward* in the New Testament literally means to *pay for service (Strong's Dictionary)*. Since we realize that our salvation is not something that can be earned by works (Titus 3:5; Eph. 2:8-9), it may come as a surprise to learn how often the Scriptures characterize the joys of heaven as a *reward*.

- Jesus promised a reward in heaven to those who are willing to suffer persecution for His name. He said, "Blessed are you when they revile and persecute you, and say all kinds

of you when they revile and persecute you, and say all kinds of evil against you falsely for My sake. Rejoice and be exceedingly glad, for **great is your reward in heaven**" (Matt. 5:11-12a).

- The book of Hebrews teaches us that holding on to our confidence in Christ has *great reward*, and that by doing the will of God with endurance we may receive it. "Therefore do not cast away your confidence, which has **great reward.** For you have need of endurance, so that after you have done the will of God, you may receive the promise" (Heb. 10:35-36).

- Paul told servants to do their work "as to the Lord and not to men, knowing that from the Lord you will receive the **reward of the inheritance**" (Col. 3:23-24).

So, the Scriptures definitely depict heaven as a reward, and while that may surprise us, it probably shouldn't. Our Father expects His children to behave, and the reward of heaven is used to motivate us to do so.

But heaven is no mere bribe. Entrance into heaven is a consequence – a consequence of what God has done for us, and of the faith and love that we have toward Him in return. The Lord desires to grant a heavenly inheritance to all men; in fact, He has done everything He can do to make that possible. He merely asks us to respond to Him in faith and love. But let no one deceive you. *Faith works* and *love labors* (1 Thess. 1:3). Those who refuse to labor for the Lord show themselves to be unappreciative of all that He has done to open the way to heaven, and they are therefore unqualified to receive it.

## WORKING TO BE REWARDED

My father was a sergeant in the U.S. Army. When I was growing up, he would often assign me chores. And whether it was cleaning my room, washing the car, working in the garden, or painting the house, I could count on there being a good old fashioned army inspection when my work was finished. I expected to be inspected! Praise or punishment would be doled out accordingly. It motivated me to do my work according to his standards.

Even so, there will be a day in which our Lord will examine our works and determine our reward. In the last day we will be judged according to our works! Jesus said that, "The Son of Man will come in the glory of His Father with His angels, and then He **will reward each according to his works**" (Matt. 16:27). He promised, "I am coming quickly, and My **reward** is with Me, to **give to every one according to his work**" (Rev. 22:12). At the great judgment scene depicted in Revelation 20:12-13, John saw "the dead, small and great, standing before God, and books were opened. And another book was opened, which is the Book of Life. And the dead **were judged according to their works**, by the things which were written in the books. The sea gave up the dead who were in it, and Death and Hades delivered up the dead who were in them. And they were judged, **each one according to his works**."

The day of our surprise inspection is coming. Jesus counsels us to "Watch therefore, for you know neither the day nor the hour in which the Son of Man is coming" (Matt. 25:13). So, you better watch out! Almost reminds you of a Christmas song, doesn't it? But while parents may go ahead and give their children their gifts even if the kids have been bad, rest assured that the Lord will not. "Watch yourselves, so that you may not lose what we have worked for, but may win a full reward" (2 John 8, ESV).

WORKING TO BE REMEMBERED

At the judgment day, each of us will receive the consequences of our actions in this life. "For we must all appear before the judgment seat of Christ, that each one may receive the things done in the body, according to what he has done, whether good or bad" (2 Cor. 5:10).

The thorough nature of this judgment indicates that the Lord will have a comprehensive record of everything we have done. The only human activity absent from that record will be the sins which God Himself has forgiven and mercifully blotted out. Since we recognize that "all have sinned," it eases the mind to know that the Lord in His mercy and grace would do this! He says, "I, even

I, am He who blots out your transgressions for My own sake; and I will not remember your sins" (Isa. 43:24).

Our one hope for good standing on the Judgment Day rests in the mercy of God in expunging the record of our sins. Like King David, each of us in our hearts pleads, "Have mercy upon me, O God, according to Your loving kindness; according to the multitude of Your tender mercies, blot out my transgressions" (Ps. 51:1). This is what we need. But how can we obtain it? The apostle Peter answers that question in Acts 3:19 when he commands, "Repent therefore and be converted, that your sins may be blotted out, so that times of refreshing may come from the presence of the Lord" (Acts 3:19). Having an unsullied record on the Day of Judgment requires that we turn from our sins and allow ourselves to be converted into the image of God's Son.

If our sins are blotted out by God's grace in this way, all that will remain on our record will be the good that we have done to honor our Lord in this life. Those who respected God and served Him in the days of Malachi were assured that this is how their record would read.

> *"Then those who feared the LORD spoke to one another,*
> *and the LORD listened and heard them; So a book of*
> *remembrance was written before Him for those who fear*
> *the LORD and who meditate on His name. 'They shall be Mine,'*
> *says the LORD of hosts, 'On the day that I make them My jewels.*
> *And I will spare them as a man spares his own son who serves*
> *him.' Then you shall again discern between the righteous and the*
> *wicked, between one who serves God*
> *and one who does not serve Him" (Mal. 3:16-18).*

How wondrous it would be to stand before the Lord on the last day and be received as a son – remembered for obedience and not for transgression.

One of the great people of faith in the Old Testament is Nehemiah. Most Bible students recognize him as the one responsible for rebuilding the walls of Jerusalem after the children of Israel returned from Babylonian captivity. Nehemiah had been the cupbearer of the Persian King Artaxerxes. At Nehemiah's request, the king sent him back to Jerusalem to rebuild it. Under

Nehemiah's leadership, the city walls were built in an amazing fifty-two days (Neh. 6:15).

However, Nehemiah's greatest achievement may not have been in the stone and mortar of that wall which provided protection for God's people against their enemies. He worked unceasingly to encourage the Jews to obey the God of heaven. His labor was not just for their physical security, but for their spiritual security. Four times in the book that bears his name, Nehemiah asked God to remember him for what he had done.

- After describing how he provided for the Jews from his own table at great personal sacrifice, Nehemiah says, "Remember me, my God, for good, according to all that I have done for this people" (Neh. 5:19).

- After reinstating the tithes for the Levites so that they might return to serving God in the temple, Nehemiah says, "Remember me, O my God, concerning this, and do not wipe out my good deeds that I have done for the house of my God, and for its services!" (Neh. 13:14).

- After he had gone to great lengths to ensure that the Sabbath was properly sanctified, Nehemiah pleads, "Remember me, O my God, concerning this also, and spare me according to the greatness of Your mercy!" (Neh. 13:22).

- After cleansing the children of Israel "from everything pagan" and reestablishing the offerings, Nehemiah says, "Remember me, O my God, for good!" (Neh. 13:31).

Like Nehemiah, it is surely our hearts' desire that God would remember us for whatever good He has enabled us to do. The thing about God is that, while He may in His mercy forget your sins, He will never forget your righteous works. His memory is forever and "the righteous will be in everlasting remembrance" (Ps. 112:6). The Bible promises that "God is not unjust to forget your work and labor of love which you have shown toward His name..." (Heb. 6:10).

The apostle Paul stated that his hope, joy, and crown of rejoicing "in the presence of our Lord Jesus Christ at His coming" was essentially the fruit of his labor in the gospel – the saved souls of those he had worked to bring to Jesus (1 Thess. 2:19-20). He worked hard to bring others to Jesus. He said, "To this end I also labor, striving according to His working which works in me mightily" (Col. 1:29). His assurance that the reward of a "crown of righteousness" was in store for him was based on the fact that he had fought a good fight, finished his race, and kept the faith (2 Tim. 4:7-8).

One day you will stand before the Judge of all the earth trusting not only in His mercy to have forgotten your sins, but also trusting in His memory to recall the good you have done on this earth. You will stand with joy and confidence on that day if, like Paul, you have labored with all your might in this life to be remembered well by Him.

## REMEMBERED IN PARADISE

In Luke 23:42-43, a thief was dying on a cross next to Jesus. In what was very likely the last wish of a dying man, he said to Jesus, "Lord, remember me when You come into Your kingdom." And Jesus said to him, "Assuredly, I say to you, today you will be with Me in Paradise." What greater aspiration could one have than to be remembered by the Lord and be with Him in paradise? What greater tragedy could one experience than to hear Him say, "I never knew you; depart from Me"? (Matt. 7:23).

The word *paradise* actually comes to us from the Persians. Nehemiah, who also wanted to be remembered by the Lord, may well have heard it spoken while he served the king of Persia. *Paradise* is a compound word derived from "para" meaning "around" and "daeza" which means "a wall." *Paradise* referred to "a wall enclosing a garden or orchard," similar perhaps to an English garden (*American Heritage Dictionary*). We use it today to refer to a place of great natural beauty, usually in a warm and inviting climate.

The word *paradise* is found exactly three times in the Bible, and each occurrence brings us closer to understanding what paradise really is.

In 2 Corinthians 12:3-5, Paul speaks of knowing a man who was "caught up into Paradise and heard inexpressible words." He goes on to say that, "Of such a one I will boast; yet of myself I will not boast, except in my infirmities." For Paul, paradise was such a place of wonder and blessedness that he was overflowing with boastful exuberance just to know that a brother got to experience it. Our hearts are overwhelmed in a similar way when, by faith, we come to realize that such a place as paradise truly exists, and that its glories may be experienced by those who are beloved in Christ.

Paradise is also pictured in Scripture as a beautiful realm of light and peace enclosed by a glorious wall (Rev. 21:11-20). There is a crystal clear river flowing from the throne of God, and in the midst of it all there is the tree of life (Rev. 22:1-2). Jesus promises that "To him who overcomes I will give to eat from the tree of life, which is in the midst of the Paradise of God" (Rev. 2:7). Notice that paradise is the reward promised to "him who overcomes." It is those who "do His commandments" who "have the right to the tree of life, and may enter through the gates into the city" (Rev. 22:14).

The most defining characteristic of paradise is simply that it is where Jesus is. Jesus promised the thief "today you will be with Me in Paradise." In this context, paradise appears to refer to the realm of departed righteous souls. It is one of two compartments in *hades,* the place where the dead await judgment. In hades, evil men are in a state of torment, and righteous men are in bliss.

The situation of the ungodly in hades is somewhat like that of a modern-day criminal who must await his trial in prison, only to be judged guilty and sent back to prison. The same basic concept is found in the story of the rich man and Lazarus. Immediately after death, the rich man was in "torment," but Lazarus was in "Abraham's bosom" (Luke 16:19-31).

Jesus went to hades after His death, to the compartment He called paradise, but His soul was not left there because He rose from the dead (Acts 2:27-31). The promise Jesus made to the thief on the cross was essentially that the thief would be *with Him.*

Paradise isn't just a peaceful place to visit on a short vacation. It's not just a cabin on the lake or an enclosed garden where you can retreat in solitude to get away from it all. Rather, it is a place of unparalleled beauty and glory, illuminated by the very presence of the Son of God. To be with Jesus in His glory is paradise.

As a boy, I lived with my family on the island of Okinawa, a place that many would consider to be a tropical paradise. I remember the palm trees and banana trees, the villagers in their rice patties, the fields of sugar cane, the cherry blossoms on the mountainside, and the beautiful beaches. Our home sat right on the shore. In fact, a coral reef came up to our back yard. I would lie awake at night and watch out my bedroom window as the octopus fisherman floated their little boats over the reef at high tide. The lanterns in the boats looked like stars floating on the water. I was only six years old, so I wasn't allowed to go out on the reef by myself. But I still remember days when dad would take me by the hand and say, "Let's go." And we would walk along the shore, and wade out into tidal pools where purple starfish dotted the reef, and long spiny sea urchins inched along the bottom, and Nemo and Dori swam in the shallows. I can still smell the sea air, and feel the wind in my face, and the warmth of my daddy's hand. That was paradise to me.

But someday, maybe someday soon, those walks along the reef from my childhood will fade into memories grey and dim, and perhaps I'll awake in a land that is evergreen and find myself walking along the shores of eternity on a golden street beside a crystal river. And there I will come face to face with my Savior at last. And my mind will be consumed with just one concern. There will be but one thing that matters. My only thought will be to ask just this one pressing question: "Remember me?"

May our lives be utterly occupied with work that will be remembered well and rewarded graciously by our Lord!

QUESTIONS

1. Define the word *reward*.

2. Are the saved promised a reward in heaven?

3. Jesus promised to reward us according to what? (Matt. 16:27; Rev. 22:12; 20:12-13)

4. On what basis does God blot out our sins from His remembrance?

5. What is God faithful to remember? (Ps. 112:6; Heb. 6:10)

6. For what did Nehemiah want God to remember him? (Neh. 5:19; 13:14, 22, 31)

7. What is *paradise*?

8. Who has a right to the tree of life in paradise? (Rev. 2:7; 22:14)

9. **Thought Questions for private reflection:**

   - What would you like the Lord to forget about your life?

   - What would you like the Lord to remember about your life?

   - What should you be doing if you want the Lord to remember you well in paradise?

*Chapter Nine*

# $\mathcal{H}$elp from $\mathcal{H}$eaven

In 2008 an inspiring story emerged from the world of girls college softball. The Associated Press news story reads...

*"With two runners on base and a strike against her, Sara Tucholsky of Western Oregon University uncorked her best swing and did something she had never done, in high school or college. Her first home run cleared the center-field fence.*

*But it appeared to be the shortest of dreams come true when she missed first base, started back to tag it and collapsed with a knee injury.*

*She crawled back to first but could do no more. The first-base coach said she would be called out if her teammates tried to help her. Or, the umpire said, a pinch runner could be called in, and the homer would count as a single.*

*Then, members of the Central Washington University softball team stunned spectators by carrying Tucholsky around the bases Saturday so the three-run homer would count — an act that contributed to their own elimination from the playoffs.*

*Central Washington first baseman Mallory Holtman, the career home run leader in the Great Northwest Athletic Conference, asked the umpire if she and her teammates could help Tucholsky. The umpire said there was no rule against it.*

*So Holtman and shortstop Liz Wallace put their arms under Tucholsky's legs, and she put her arms over their shoulders. The three headed around the base paths, stopping to let Tucholsky touch each base with her good leg.*

*"The only thing I remember is that Mallory asked me which leg was the one that hurt," Tucholsky said. "I told her it was my right leg, and she said, 'OK, we're going to drop you down gently*

*and you need to touch it with your left leg,' and I said 'OK, thank you very much.'"*

*"She said, 'You deserve it, you hit it over the fence,' and we all kind of just laughed."*

*"We started laughing when we touched second base,"*
*Holtman said. "I said, 'I wonder what this must look like to other people."'*

*"We didn't know that she was a senior or that this was her first home run," Wallace said Wednesday. "That makes the story more touching than it was. We just wanted to help her."*

*..."In the end, it is not about winning and losing so much,"*
*Holtman said. "It was about this girl. She hit it over the fence and was in pain, and she deserved a home run."*

That great story has some wonderful parallels to think about as we run toward our heavenly home. We can't make it home on our own. We need help. But in our case, we don't deserve a home run and there will certainly be no help from the opposing team! Satan IS NOT about helping us. So, our help has to come from heaven, and let me tell you, it is abundant!

## "UNDERNEATH ARE THE EVERLASTING ARMS"

Our journey is not one we make alone. The Lord Himself will help us. From a Roman prison, the Apostle Paul wrote to encourage Christians, saying he was "confident of this very thing, that **He who has begun a good work in you will complete it** until the day of Christ Jesus" (Phil. 1:6). He encourages them to "work out your own salvation" (which means to see it through to the end) and then adds *"for it is God who works in you both to will and to do for His good pleasure"* (Phil. 2:13). The Father, Son and Holy Spirit are ever working, and I am cooperating (Eph. 3:14-21).

Even in the toughest trials of life, God will be with us, His arms underneath helping us toward home.

*"The eternal God is your refuge,*
*And **underneath are the everlasting arms**;*
*He will thrust out the enemy before you, and will say, 'Destroy!'"*
(Deut. 33:27)

This is what Paul found true for his life. When no one else stood with him, he says, **"But the Lord stayed with me and strengthened me."** God delivered him out of the mouth of the lion, and confidence explodes as Paul concludes, "And the Lord will deliver me from every evil work and preserve me for His heavenly kingdom. To Him be glory forever and ever. Amen" (2 Tim. 4:16-18).

God does not promise that bad things will never happen in our lives. What He does promise is that He will be with us, always helping, never leaving us or forsaking us (Heb. 13:5-6). He will work for ultimate good in His amazing providence (Romans 8:28). There is help from above!

## NEVER A BUSY SIGNAL

Perhaps the greatest help God gives us as we run toward home is the ability to talk to Him and listen to Him. And get this...there's is never a busy signal when those who love Him want to reach Him. He never sleeps nor slumbers (Psa. 121:4). Elijah once mocked the Baal worshippers suggesting Baal was busy. He added, "Perhaps he is sleeping and must be awakened" (1 Kings 18:26-27). False gods have ears but they can't hear (Psa. 115:4-8). God is always available and eager to hear His children (1 Pet. 3:12).

Sometimes I am asked, "What is most vital in being a strong Christian?" My answer always is, "Pray to God every day. Read your Bible every day. Think about who you are and where you are spiritually every day." It sounds simple I know, but it's true. Here is your field radio to your Commander in the midst of war! When you pray, you are talking to God. When you read your Bible, you are listening to God.

These daily habits are often called "Private Disciplines." The name fits for it takes discipline to do them, and they are done in private. God does great surgery on us here. Solitude has been compared to an anesthetic that puts everything to sleep before surgery can take place. But I'm afraid too many of us Christians are not doing these things. One reason may be we have not learned to be comfortable with quietness. We most always want radios on in the car and TVs on in the house. Not good. Another reason may be sheer laziness, and we need to learn to exercise "mind over mattress." Maybe neither of those are true, and we simply think we are too busy to stop and do it.

Traveling to heaven is a daily journey. We take one day at a time, and with each passing day our salvation is nearer than when we first believed (Rom. 13:11). The way we begin each day is crucial. The first action of the day tends to rule the day. Prayer, Bible reading, and meditation have a way of staying with you, reminding you of who you are, Whom you serve, and where you are headed. I've always loved the words of Ralph Cushman in "I Met God In The Morning."

*I met God in the morning*
*when the day was at its best,*
*And His Presence came like sunrise,*
*Like a glory in my breast.*

*All day long the Presence lingered,*
*All day long He stayed with me,*
*And we sailed in perfect calmness,*
*O'er a very troubled sea.*

*Other ships were blown and battered,*
*Other ships were sore distressed,*
*But the winds that seemed to drive them,*
*Brought to me a peace and rest.*

*Then I thought of other mornings,*
*With a keen remorse of mind,*
*When I too had loosed the moorings,*
*With the presence left behind.*

*So, I think I know the secret,*
*Learned from many a troubled way:*
*You must seek Him in the morning*
*If you want Him through the day!*

So, find you a quiet place and talk to God. That's what prayer is. It is simply sitting before the Lord (2 Sam. 7:18). You don't even have to speak out loud. God can understand it from your heart. Just ask Hannah. She "spoke in her heart; only her lips moved but her voice was not heard" (1 Sam. 1:13). Sometimes we don't even have the words to express what we are feeling, but we have help in those moments. I would rather have heart with no words, than words with no heart. Don't hold anything back. Pour out your soul (1 Sam. 1:15).

The Bible teaches that the Holy Spirit understands what we are trying to say and makes intercession for us (Rom. 8:26-27). He works much like the mother of a two-year-old who knows her child intimately and is easily able to tell others what her child is trying to say, even though he doesn't quite have the words. What a blessing He is to us when we groan through our prayers!

You need a time for both *"closet prayers"* and *"arrow prayers."* Jesus spoke of closet prayers where you actually have time and take time to go into your room (Matt. 6:6). Nehemiah obviously prayed an "arrow prayer" where he offered a quick but well-aimed shot toward heaven (Neh. 2:4). Sometimes we need to talk to God on the spot, and we can't run off to a private room. Using these two types of prayers, we can have continual lines of communication to God. We can "pray without ceasing" (1 Thess. 5:17). This doesn't mean you are always talking to God but it does mean the line is always open. It's similar to my travels with my wife. We talk along the way, sometimes get quiet for a little while, but we are still connected, and when we need to say something again, we do.

Also, read your Bible asking yourself how you need to apply what you are reading. Examine yourself (2 Cor. 13:5). Ask God in His word to show you areas where you should improve (Psa. 139:23-24). Your Bible is a spiritual GPS. It will **show you where you are** spiritually, **where you need to go**, and **how to get there**. After receiving all of that 411, you simply **"Go."**

Meditate on your relationship with God throughout the day. And be sure to bring God into every activity of your life. Our lives are not cut up like pie slices making sure we have a piece of our life that says "God." He will not accept being a piece of your pie.

Twenty four/seven, He is the pie, the whole of our lives (Eccl. 12:13-14)!

## ARMOR FROM HEAVEN

Another help from heaven is armor to fight against the devil. I fear that too many Christians do not live with a war mentality. Ever since man was created, there has been a war for our souls. Eden is our ground zero. God loves us and wants us with Him eternally. Satan hates God and, therefore, comes after God's most treasured possession, His people. He is also operating on the principle of "misery loves company." The devil knows his eternal destiny and is working to take as many with him as he can (Rev. 20:10).

This is not a walk in the park. **We are at war!** We don't choose if we will be involved; the war has come to us. In essence, the devil has a war room where he schemes and devises a fine-tuned plan for destroying you and me (2 Cor. 2:11). He's a wily one (Ephesians 6:11). He also has a film room of sorts where he watches tapes of us playing the game of life. He's not omniscient like God. He doesn't have to be. He just watches us and at some point says, "Ah hah! There's a weak spot." And he attacks it. Our job is to leave no unguarded place.

What we need then is a special suit of armor, and God provides it, and we must suit up every morning when we rise. Ephesians 6:10-20 is God's armory. Repeatedly, God tells us to suit up, stand, and depend on the Lord's strength, not our own. We sing, *"Stand up, stand up for Jesus. Stand in His strength alone. The arm of flesh will fail you; Ye dare not trust your own."* Read your Old Testament and see the many times God made it clear to His people that to win they must trust in His strength, not theirs (2 Chron. 32:8). What follows is a list of each piece of armor with a brief description:

- **Waist girded with truth** (vs. 14). The whole suit of armor is bound at the middle. Our core is strong with God's truth. The devil cannot defeat *"It is written"* (Matt. 4:1-11). The rest of the world may walk dizzily around saying, "What is truth?"; but not us.

- **A breastplate of righteousness** (vs. 14). We are committed and strong in our resolve to *do right*. But also, we have strength to fight because we know we *are right* with God having our sins cleansed in the blood of Christ (Rom. 3:21-26). It's hard to win a battle if you think you are already defeated going into it.

- **Feet shod with the preparation of the gospel of peace** - Footwear is everything in battle. Our feet are made strong to *advance the gospel of peace* because we already *have peace with God* (Rom. 5:1-2). He is mine. I am His. "Let's roll."

- **Shield of faith** - This large shield used by the Roman army was covered with leather and soaked in water to quench arrows dipped in pitch. The devil fires flaming missiles, but our faith, trust, and commitment to God quenches them all. Faith is the victory (1 John 5:4-5)!

- **Helmet of salvation** - Covering the seat of knowledge (our brain) is this helmet. Here is our awareness that all is well between us and God. *I am saved.* This keeps me mentally strong while I fight. Why fight if I'm already lost? This confidence (not arrogance) is crucial. We must gird up the mind (1 Pet. 1:13-16).

- **The sword of the Spirit.** Here is our **offensive** weapon. It is the *word of God.* Again, remember that Jesus used Scripture to resist and fight the devil. Satan ran (James 4:7)! Satan cannot defeat a soldier determined to stand with God and equipped to thrust him through with truth! Here's why we must know God's word. You can't fight with what you don't know!

- **Pray always with all prayer.** We sing, "Each piece put on with prayer." Stay connected to the Commander.

Here then is our armor for meeting the devil head on. Again, if we resist, he will flee from us. Arise each morning; thank God for the armor and help He gives. Suit up and be left standing when the day ends.

## CHEERING SUPPORTERS IN THE GRANDSTANDS

As we make our run toward heaven God has given us people who in essence cheer for us. They are those people of great faith in the Bible whom we've read about, and who have inspired us. They have run their race, finished it; and now sit in the grandstands cheering for us as we run. I believe this is the amazing picture we have in Hebrews 12:1-2.

Chapter 11 has just laid before us men and women of great faith who kept pursuing what they could not see. They never forfeited the invisible for the visible. This is what we all must do. We must **see the unseen** and never forget that the most real and lasting things are the things we cannot see (2 Cor. 4:16 - 5:8). Having been inspired by these heroes in the hall of faith and others we read about elsewhere, we find the following in chapter 12:

*"Therefore we also, since we are*
*surrounded by so great a cloud of witnesses,*
*let us lay aside every weight,*
*and the sin which so easily ensnares us,*
*and let us run with endurance the race that is set before us,*
*looking unto Jesus, the author and finisher of our faith,*
*who for the joy that was set before Him*
*endured the cross, despising the shame,*
*and has sat down at the right hand of the throne of God.*
*For consider Him who endured such hostility from sinners against*
*Himself, lest you become weary and discouraged in your souls.*
*You have not yet resisted to bloodshed, striving against sin."*
(Heb. 12:1-4)

So, in the grandstands is a great cloud of witnesses who have crossed the finished line, and they now cheer for us. We don't have to outrun anyone else, we just have to finish! The Bible talks a lot about finishing, with Jesus being the "finisher of our faith" (Heb. 12:2).

Not only do these supporters want us to finish; they remove all our excuses for never entering the race or for failing to finish. We may try to say, *"I couldn't see any evidence for God. How can you expect me to believe in an invisible God?"* But we look and see **Moses** in the stands who saw and followed an invisible God (Heb. 11:24-27). Even God says the agnostic and the atheist are without excuse (Rom. 1:20). We say, *"Sexual temptation was just too strong, I couldn't be faithful."* But then we catch a glimpse of **Joseph** who resisted daily temptation to be sexually impure (Gen. 39). We offer up *"It was just too hard. I couldn't do it,"* and there is **Abraham,** who in faithful obedience, went to sacrifice his only son. Talk about hard! Or perhaps we bring a broken-hearted, humble spirit and say, *"I've just done too many bad things in my life. God could never forgive me. I can't come to Him."* And we hear **David** in the stands shouting, "Blessed are those whose lawless deeds are forgiven" (Rom. 4:7)! He's the very man who in one chapter of his life broke six of the ten commandments including taking another man's wife and then murdering her husband. Talk about bad!

See my point? **There's no excuse for not entering and finishing this race.** We have supporters in the stands; some of whom we don't even know! They take away our excuses and say to us, "Yes, you can" (Heb. 11:36-40)! They finished. We can too.

Now look up to the Chief seat in the arena. Who do you see? There's **Jesus**. No one faced a more hostile crowd than Jesus. The opposing team offered Him no help in getting around the bases and on to home. But regardless, He made the final stride home! With freshly moistened lips and a freed tongue, He cried out with a loud voice on the cross, **"It is finished"** (John 19:28-30). We must look to Him and finish! And when we finish, we can run up to our King and receive not a fading crown of laurel but a crown of life (Rev. 2:10). What a joy to hear Him one day say, "Well done!"

Hebrews 11 is not all we have. There are others spread throughout the Bible who inspire us. I remember a brother in Christ who asked his suffering sister how he could help her, and she responded, "My brother, tell me about Job. Tell me about Job."

Even Jesus was supplied with such helpers. With the cross looming on the horizon, who appeared to Him? Moses and Elijah. What were they talking about? His approaching death - His *exodus* from this wilderness (Luke 9:30-31). Like Elijah, He would soon be set free from earth's prison bars and fly away. I don't know what they said but I am certain just seeing these two finishers encouraged Jesus!

The bottom line? We have God-given supporters to push us onward - help from heaven!

## COMRADES & CONSCIENCE

Our helpers are not just those on the other side; there are also fellow Christians here below who help us. God knew we needed comrades to come to our aid in life and provide encouragement to press on. That's why we have so many *"one another"* passages in the Bible. We don't go at this alone.

Few Christians have faced greater trials than the apostle Paul (2 Cor. 11:23-28), but we cannot help but feel the strength he received when brethren came to his side. In the book of Acts, sailing toward a Roman imprisonment and being beaten by storms, Paul finally found an oasis! He says, "...**we found brethren** and were invited to stay with them seven days." Brethren sacrificed to help him. "And from there, **when the brethren heard about us, they came to meet us** as far as Appi Forum and Three Inns. **When Paul saw them, he thanked God and took courage**" (Acts 28:15-16). And a gracious God from heaven made sure that even under house arrest, he "received all who came to him...no one forbidding him" (Acts 28:30-31). Brethren risked their physical health and even their necks for him (Phil. 2:25-30; Rom. 16:4).

And in our day, they call us, they send cards, they visit us, they sit with us, they prepare meals, they make long trips, they keep our children, etc. etc. etc. In all of it, their spirit proclaims, "He ain't heavy. He's my brother."

True comrades also do the hard things. When they feel they must, they come with love and a meek spirit to rebuke us when we are wrong. But if we are not careful, it can be easy not to appreciate such actions. It might not feel like friendship to us, but the truth is they are the greatest friends we have. *"Faithful are the wounds of a friend but the kisses of an enemy are deceitful"* (Prov. 27:6). It hurts. We feel wounded. But oh, what a friend! Let us not refuse it (Psa. 141:5). Paul and Peter are great examples of two loyal comrades. Peter needed correcting in Galatians 2, and Paul "withstood him to his face." Did Peter write Paul off his friend list? No! Later in life, Peter still calls him "our beloved brother Paul" (2 Pet. 3:15). All indications are that Peter's conscience kicked in; he realized he was wrong, and he changed. This leads me to discuss one final help from heaven.

Our consciences are great gifts from God. They are internal alarm systems that blare at us when we are doing wrong, and they convict us to get back on track. God didn't have to give them to us, but He obviously knew we needed them.

To work properly, we first have to program our consciences with the word of God. If a conscience is not aware of what is right and wrong, it will never sound at the needed time.

And know this. It is possible to dull our consciences and become past feeling (1 Tim. 4:2; Eph. 4:19). It's like the man who hit his thumb with a hammer, and his boss walked by, and said, "If you will do that every day, it will get where it doesn't hurt anymore." Why, of course! All the nerve endings are shot. And don't run off to some worldly counselor who works really hard to tell your conscience, "Be quiet!" Sin is still sin, and shame is healthy and God-given. Shame brings us back on track. It seems to have done that with Adam and Eve. It did with King David who committed adultery. It did with Peter who denied the Lord. It will with you. Conscience and comrades are God-given help from above.

May we all be strengthened in the Lord who is our Helper and provides all we need to circle the bases of life and arrive home at last.

## QUESTIONS

1.  Does God actually help us in our journey toward heaven? What verses so teach?

2.  How is it that there is never a busy signal when we sincerely pray to God? Why didn't Baal (an Old Testament idol) respond to his worshippers when they cried out to him?

3.  What are "Private Disciplines," and why are they so important? Do you engage in them as you should? Why or why not?

4.  Having read the chapter, what is the simplest definition you can give for prayer?

5.  What is the difference in an "arrow prayer" and a "closet prayer?" Give examples for each.

6.  Why is meditation so important?

7.  As we fight the devil, do we fight in our strength alone? What battle gear (armor) are we provided by God? List all the pieces of armor.

8.  Do you think often of the spiritual battle you fight against Satan? Why is it so important that we keep a war mindset?

9.  Where does the Bible speak of cheering supporters we have in the grandstands as we run our race? How do they help us? Who would be a great Bible character whose example has helped you greatly?

10. Why are comrades and conscience so needed in our lives?

## Chapter Ten

# *H*indrances & Obstacles

I still remember the face of Mary Decker after she tripped and fell to the curb in the 3000 meter run in the 1984 Summer Olympics. I think I saw sorrow, anguish, pain, disappointment, and anger all at once. It was a look that's hard to forget.

Decker, who was heavily favored, collided with the barefooted Zola Budd of Great Britain. Decker claimed that Budd cut in on her and was to blame for tripping her. Many sided with Decker while others claimed it was her own fault for not giving enough space. Who was to blame? Perhaps it will always be debated, but one thing I know: **the pain is unimaginable when you have trained so long and run so well and then fail to finish the race.**

## WHO HINDERED YOU?

When the apostle Paul wrote to the Christians in Galatia disappointment must have been on his face. He says to them, *"You were running a good race. Who cut in on you and kept you from obeying the truth?"* (Gal. 5:7 - NIV). I love the rendering "Who cut in on you?". The New King James reads, *"You ran well. Who hindered you...?"* I'm pretty sure I know the answer. I think Paul gives us the answer in another place where he says, "Therefore, we wanted to come to you - even I, Paul, time and again - but **Satan hindered us**" (1 Thess. 2:18).

That says it all. As we run the race toward heaven there is a great enemy who strives to trip us up. His name is Satan, and his name means "the adversary." He hates God and has been man's enemy since the very beginning. He knows that God has set his heart on a man's victory, and more than anything he wants to take the smile off the face of God. Oh, it may seem at times that our enemy is some other person, but don't be fooled; there is an enemy behind the scenes.

**"For we do not wrestle against flesh and blood,**
but against principalities, against powers,
against the rulers of the darkness of this age,
**against spiritual hosts of wickedness in the heavenly places."**
(Eph. 6:12)

"Be sober, be vigilant;
because **your adversary the devil**,
walks about like a roaring lion,
**seeking whom he may devour."**
(1 Pet. 5:8)

I'm persuaded he is operating on the principle of "misery loves company." If he can read, and I think he can, then he surely knows his ultimate destiny is hell (Rev. 20:10). He would love to take as many as he can with him when he goes.

You and I must know that the path we travel will have hindrances and obstacles along the way. The good news is that God has told us what they will be. When it comes to Satan, *"...we are not ignorant of his devices"* (2 Cor. 2:11). But beware! While God has lovingly told us what the devil's devices are, they still work on too many people. For that reason, Satan has no new tricks. The old ones will do.

The devil is a wily one, and he will meet in the war room to devise a scheme for taking you out of the contest (Ephesians 6:11). So be prepared. Take the B-I-B-L-E, which a friend of mine says is **"B**asic **I**nstructions **B**efore **L**eaving **E**arth." Take your stand on it.

Space does not allow us to discuss all the hindrances and obstacles along the way. God has done that in His word. But we will set forth a few of the common ones we see quite often.

# FALSE TEACHING

Beloved brother Irven Lee used to say, "For every verse you give me on any Bible subject, I can give you one on false teaching. And when you have finished, I will still be giving you verses on false teaching." His point is spot on! The Bible constantly warns us about those who teach error.

The devil is a liar. He always has been (John 8:44). He loves to place a lie right beside the truth. He did in the Garden of Eden and has ever since. In the garden, God plainly told Adam and Eve that if they ate of the tree of knowledge of good and evil, *"You shall surely die"* (Gen. 2:17). The serpent, the devil of old, said *"You will **not** surely die"* (Gen. 3:4). Well, there it is. Truth and a lie...side-by-side. And Eve chose the lie.

Please notice that all the devil had to do was insert a little but BIG word. It was the word "not." Someone once called it "The 'Not' in the Devil's Tale." Satan creates a lie easily by either adding or deleting a "not." He's done it in today's world too. The religious world teaches that we are saved by *"faith only."* But the Bible clearly says, *"**not** by faith only"* (James 2:24). See the old trick? In the garden, Satan added a "not." In this case, he takes out the "not." Here again is truth and a lie side-by-side. Which do you believe? God allows them to be side-by-side to give you choice and to test your love and loyalty to Him and His word. Don't get tripped up!

Satan has preachers too (2 Cor. 11:13-15). They can put on coats and ties, hold Bibles in their hands, and talk so smoothly and convincingly, yet all the while preaching a lie. Some do it deliberately; others do it unintentionally and with sincerity, but the result is the same. People are led astray from the truth.

How do you protect yourself from false teachers? It's simple. Get your Bible off the shelf, read it for yourself, and examine every teaching under the microscope of God's word. The best way to spot a counterfeit is to handle the real thing all the time. Test the spirits (1 John 4:1). Prove all things (1 Thess. 5:21). Don't fall for old lies that sound good on the surface but simply are not true. Dig deep in God's word. The devil knows if you preach a lie long enough, people will come to believe it's true. An unknown author once penned, "It is easier to believe a lie one has heard a thousand times than to believe a fact one has never heard before." Be like the Bereans of old...

> *"These were more fair minded than those in Thessalonica, in that they searched the Scriptures daily to find out whether these things were so."*
> (Acts 17:11)

## TRIALS & TRIBULATIONS

One of Satan's greatest devices to lead people off the path to heaven is discouragement. Too many people think that once they become Christians their life will be free of problems. It's not true. Jesus faced some of His fiercest temptations *after* his baptism (Matt. 4). And He knew that if we are not forewarned about trials and tribulations, we might become disillusioned and quickly fall away. In the parable of the sower, speaking of the stony ground, He taught:

> *"These likewise are the ones sown on stony ground who, when they hear the word of God, immediately receive it with gladness; and they have no root in themselves, and so endure for a time. Afterward when tribulation or persecution arises for the word's sake, immediately they stumble."*
> (Mark 4:15-16)

Of course, no one loves trials and tribulations, but we can learn to take joy in them once we understand what's going on. Yes, Satan uses trials trying to discourage us and destroy our faith. Yet, God allows the trial to test our mettle and produce spiritual muscle. There's a difference in *tempting* and *testing*. Satan tempts; God never does (James 1:12-16).

We are headed to a place where there are no tears, sorrow, or pain, but the road that leads there is paved with them (Acts 14:21-22). When we **know** that God allows trials to produce spiritual strength in us we can actually have joy in those times. It's not a giddy happiness but a deep satisfying joy that God is working for good. The key is in what you **know**. See the emphasized words in these two verses.

> *"My brethren, count it all joy*
> *when you fall into various trials,*
> ***knowing that*** *the testing of your faith*
> *produces patience. But let patience have its*
> *perfect work, that you may be complete, lacking nothing."*
> (James 1:2-4)

> *"And not only that, but we also glory in tribulations,*
> ***knowing that*** *tribulation produces perseverance;*
> *and perseverance, character; and character, hope."*
> (Rom. 5:3-4)

Sometimes you will be able to see wonderful things God accomplished for you or someone else in your trials. At other times, it may make no sense at all. In those moments, just **let God be God**. *"Let Him do what seems good to him"* (1 Sam. 3:18). Tie a knot in the rope, hang on, and never let go.

There's a modern-day story I love to tell that illustrates the truth on how God uses our trials, temptations, and hardships to strengthen us. It's the story of a man told by God to push a rock. He pushes day after day from sunup to sundown and then grows discouraged because the rock never budges. He cries out to God about it, and God responds. *"My friend, when long ago I asked you to serve Me, and you accepted, I told you to push against the rock with all your strength, and that you have done. But never once did I mention to you that I expected you to move it. At least not by yourself. Your task was to push. And now you come to Me, your strength spent, thinking that you have failed, ready to quit. But is this really so? Look at yourself. Your arms are strong and muscled; your back sinewed and brown. Your hands are calloused from constant pressure, and your legs have become massive and hard. Through opposition you have grown much and your ability now far surpasses that which you used to have. Yet still, you haven't succeeded in moving the rock, and you come to Me now with a heavy heart and your strength spent. I, my friend will move the rock. Your calling was to be obedient and push, and to exercise your faith and trust in My wisdom, and this you have done."*

Press through trials and tribulations; they lead home!!

## CARES, RICHES, AND PLEASURES OF THIS LIFE

In the Parable of the Sower, Jesus said that some of the seed *"fell among thorns, and the thorns sprang up with it and choked it"* (Luke 8:7). Lord, what are these thorns? *"And the ones that fell among thorns are those who, when they have heard, go out and are choked with cares, riches, and pleasures of life and bring no fruit to maturity"* (Luke 8:14).

Too many of us Christians are thorny ground. Ouch! I think I've got thorns wrapped on me too! We would read the Bible daily, pray, meditate, and talk to others about Christ, but we don't feel like we have the time. If we are too busy to do those things, then we are simply TOO BUSY! I personally believe it is our #1 problem in the church today.

There was a day when more people lived a "Little House on the Prairie" lifestyle but now it has been replaced with "A Big House on the Freeway." People are living hectic lives, and a lot of it is because they have come down with "Affluenza." Yes, you heard me right. "Affluenza," not "influenza," has become a national epidemic as people chase the American Dream instead of the heavenly dream.

Lives are lived louder, but emptier. And most are not really satisfied. The itch is not getting scratched (Eccl. 2:1-11). That's because what we really need is being ignored every day. Jesus gets buried beneath cares, riches, and pleasures of this life. Thorns are wrapped all around us and we are choking!

What's the solution to the problem? Downsize. Get some pruning shears and start cutting away the thorns. Prioritize your life. Make God's agenda your agenda. Get on the same page with Him. I believe more of us need to strive for what some have called "the middle way." It's talked about and prayed about in Proverbs.

*"Two things I request of You*
*(Deprive me not before I die)*
*remove falsehood and lies from me;*

*give me neither poverty nor riches -*
*feed me with the food that you prescribe for me;*
*Lest I be full and deny You,*
*and say, "Who is the Lord?"*
*Or lest I be poor and steal,*
*and profane the name of my God."*
(Prov. 30:7-9)

The wise man is saying, "I don't want too much. I don't want too little. I just ask for enough." The problem is too many of us don't know when to say "It's enough" (Luke 12:16-21). Don't trip on a brier!

## BAD FRIENDS

I cannot tell you how the rest of your life will go. But I can tell you that a lot of it will depend on the kinds of friends you choose. They will make you or break you.

I'm thinking of Amnon, David's son. The Bible simply says, *"Amnon had a friend"* (2 Samuel 13:3). Of course he did. We all do.

The text says that Amnon loved his sister Tamar. Lust is more like it. But it was "improper for Amnon to do anything to her" (13:2). That just might be one of the greatest understatements in the Bible.

But since Amnon has a friend, I'm sure he will help him to overcome this terrible temptation. He didn't. He counseled Amnon to go to his bedroom, pretend as if he were sick, call Tamar to come assist her poor brother, and then make his move. And that's exactly what Amnon did. When she refused, he raped her (13:11-14). How's that for a friend?

A good friend is as follows:

- **Someone who will strive to deter you from doing something you know is wrong** (1 Sam. 25:32-35).

- **Someone who will lovingly rebuke you when you have done wrong** (2 Samuel 12).

- **Someone who will encourage you to go ahead and do what you already know is right** (2 Kings 5:13).

- **Someone who will teach you the truth when you are in error** (Acts 18:24-26).

You do not have to choose bad friends. There are good ones out there. You just have to go to the right places to find them. And the greatest news of all is that Christians always have a friend. His name is Jesus (John 15:13).

> *"Jesus is all the world to me,*
> *I want no better friend;*
> *I trust Him now, I'll trust him when*
> *Life's fleeting day's shall end;*
> *Beautiful life with such a friend;*
> *Beautiful life that has no end.*
> *Eternal life, eternal joy,*
> *He's my friend."*
> (Will L. Thompson)

## BITTERNESS TOWARD GOD & OTHERS

Too many people quit serving the Lord because they become bitter toward God. Something happens in their life that is devastating, and they turn against Him. Job's wife did. In the midst of all his trials, she encouraged him to curse God and die (Job 2:9). I realize she was hurting too but those were terrible words that could have made Job bitter too. But Job, while questioning things and sometimes speaking wrong things, never let go of God. And God never let go of him. And at the end of Job's life, we see that God was very merciful (James 5:11). Trust Him.

I think too of Naomi, who said to her friends, *"Do not call me Naomi; call me Mara for the Almighty has dealt very bitterly with me"* (Ruth 1:20). But in both cases, God was working for a wonderful end. From Naomi's daughter-in-law, Ruth, came the Son of God! Wow! Lesson learned? Trust Him.

Then there are those who become embittered because someone else hurt them in some way. It happens. Sometimes it

92

even happens that the person who hurts you is someone you would always expect to love you; a family member or a Christian. And we run off saying something like, "If that's the way Christians act, I want no part of it." Don't do it.

Take Joseph as an example. His own brothers wanted to kill him. Instead, they threw him in a pit and, thereafter, sold him into slavery. But he never let bitterness rule him. He forgave them and even saw God's providence in it (Gen. 45:5-8).

Bitterness kills spirituality. Some of my favorite snippets are "It's not the snake biting you that does the greatest harm. It's chasing him down that drives the poison to the heart." And, "Bitterness is drinking poison and hoping someone else dies." Don't let bitterness spring up and cause trouble (Heb. 12:15).

## NOT RESPECTING THE DISTANCE

The distance of a marathon has to be respected and a cost counted by those who sign up to run. It's not a short sprint. You have to get a grip on that.

When the gun goes off, all those at the starting line look the same. But over the next 26.2 miles, some will fall by the wayside. Others will press on with great staying power. Lesson learned: *Starting power is not staying power.*

For most, the Christian life is a marathon. Very few obey the gospel and enter paradise the next day. We don't need a quick burst for a short while. We need disciplined, steady, continuous runners who watch for the things along the way that could trip them up.

Those who run marathons tell you that a great key to success is to mentally break the marathon into sections. Run from one landmark to the next. But keep running (Heb. 6:11-12). One day at a time. That's what Christians must do. The last mile will come. Finish. God will help you through every hindrance and obstacle.

> *"When I've gone the last mile of the way.*
> *I will rest at the close of the day.*
> *And I know there are joys that await me,*
> *when I've gone the last mile of the way."*
> (Johnson Oatman, Jr.)

QUESTIONS

1. When we are hindered in running the Christian race, who is behind the scenes working to trip us up? Support your answer with Scripture.

2. As stated in this chapter, what principle is the devil operating upon? Explain.

3. **Thought question:** Since the devil schemes and devises plans to cause us to fall (2 Cor. 2:11; Ephesians 6:11), what might he try with you? For private reflection only.

4. What one little word does the devil love to use to turn truth to error? Give examples.

5. What is the God-given way to protect ourselves against false teaching?

6. The phrase "knowing that" was highlighted in this chapter to teach how we should view our trials. What verses use that phrase, and what can we learn from those verses?

7. What are the dangers of cares, riches, and pleasures of life?

8. Why are good friends so important on our journey to heaven? What are some things a good friend will do for us?

9. Why do we need to guard against bitterness? Name some Bible characters who could have been bitter but did not allow it to fester in their hearts?

10. How important is endurance?

*Chapter Eleven*

# $\mathcal{P}$aint Me a $\mathcal{P}$icture

A few years ago, on the anniversary of our
wedding, I gave my wife a framed print of a painting by Marc
Chagall entitled *La Mariee* (which means *"The Bride"* in French).
The original piece sold at auction in 2011 for over one million
dollars. You might recognize it if you saw it. It depicts a bride
adorned for her husband. Chagall painted her in a full-length red
wedding gown, making her image stand out from the blue/grey
hues that surround her. Her long white veil is being held in place
by an attendant. In the background there is a church building, and
to the side there is a band playing music – an unusual band with a
man blowing what appears to be a clarinet, a goat playing a violin
and a fish acting as the conductor for the group. Strange painting,
but Sandi and I both like it.

Our own wedding was, of course, much different. And yet,
my love for my bride is wonderfully symbolized in Chagall's
work. It is not the artist's technique, the colors, or the strange
characters that make it meaningful to me; it is the focus on the
bride. She is the center of attention. She is being lovingly
attended. It is her special day, and she is happy! Who wouldn't be
happy with a fiddle-playing goat?

In Revelation 21 and 22, the inspired apostle John paints for
us a word picture of a wedding scene he was privileged to witness.
He says, "I, John, saw the holy city, New Jerusalem, coming down
out of heaven from God, **prepared as a bride adorned for her**

**husband**" (Rev. 21:2). In this chapter, we want to look closely at that painting. The images may seem strange to us, but the meaning will become clear – the bride is loved, she is beautiful, and she is eternally happy.

## THE BRIDE: SYMBOL OF THE SAVED IN HEAVEN

Few would claim that Revelation is an easy book to understand. It is filled with symbolic images which often have their roots in the history and prophecies of the Old Testament. Some of this symbolic imagery is explained in Revelation, but much of it is left to the reader to comprehend for himself. For instance, in the vision found in chapter one in which John sees one like the Son of Man in the midst of seven lampstands, we are told that the lampstands represent the seven churches of Asia (Rev. 1:11, 20). We are not told what the two-edged sword coming out of the mouth of the Son of Man represents (Rev. 1:16). But since the sword is in fact coming out of the mouth, and since the symbol of the sword is used elsewhere in Scripture to represent God's word (Heb. 4:12; Eph. 6:17), we may readily conclude that the sword represents God's word. In Revelation, Christ uses this weapon to fight against and conquer the unrepentant (Rev. 2:16; 19:15, 21).

The image of the "bride adorned for her husband" in Revelation 21 is not explained to us either. But elsewhere in Scripture the bride of Christ represents the church – the body of the saved. When Paul wrote to the Corinthian saints he said, "I have betrothed you to one husband, that I may present *you as* a chaste virgin to Christ" (2 Cor. 11:2). In Ephesians 5:25-27, the ideal relationship between a husband and wife is paralleled to the relationship between Christ and the church. Paul writes, "Husbands, love your wives, just as Christ also loved the church and gave Himself for her, that He might sanctify and cleanse her with the washing of water by the word, that He might present her to Himself a glorious church, not having spot or wrinkle or any such thing, but that she should be holy and without blemish." So, it is with much confidence that we identify the bride of Christ as the body of those who have been saved by the blood of Christ.

Some believe that the bride of Christ in Revelation 21 and 22 represents the saved on earth. While there are some aspects of the vision that lend to this interpretation, from this writer's view, most of the evidence indicates that we are being shown the saved in heaven. Whichever position is taken, nearly everyone would agree that a good bit of the symbolic language could apply equally to the saved on earth and in heaven. Some of the reasons for taking the description to apply to the saved in heaven are as follows:

- On earth, the church is the "betrothed" of Christ (2 Cor. 11:2). She is the bride to be. The marriage supper is yet future.

- In the flow of the book of Revelation, it is only after the great events of the book that the bride is said to have "made herself ready" for the marriage (Rev. 19:7-8).

- The vision of the bride in Revelation 21 occurs after the final judgment depicted in Revelation 20:11-15.

- Earlier in Revelation, Jesus had promised the church at Ephesus, "to him who overcomes I will give to eat from the tree of life" (Rev. 2:7). Obviously, access to the tree of life had not yet been given to those Christians in Ephesus. But access to the tree of life *is available* in the bride as John concludes his description of her in Revelation 22:2.

- The future tense is used predominately in the description of the bride. Notice that "he who overcomes **shall inherit** these things" (Rev. 21:7), and "those who are saved **shall walk** in its light" (Rev. 21:24; see also 21:25-27; 22:3-5).

Even as the bride herself is symbolic, so also are the details of the city that depicts her. Whether we are looking at the wall and its gates or the tree and the river which they enclose, the viewer of the painting is moved to love and appreciate the bride through these symbolic images to which we now turn our attention.

## Fellowship with God: The Destiny of the Redeemed

My grandfather and grandmother lived far away from us for most of my childhood. Maybe yours did too. I remember how much I loved them and longed to be with them. Granny would write or call occasionally. Those contacts kept us close, but made me long to be closer. I would often wonder aloud when they might come for a visit or when we might get to go see them. Of course, we had pictures and sweet memories that served to remind us of them, but there was nothing like a family vacation to my grandparents' house!

In this world, Christians enjoy many reminders of our loving, heavenly Father. We see His power and wisdom in the wonders of creation. We frequently assemble together to worship and adore Him. We communicate with Him through prayer, and He with us through His word. As wonderful as these experiences are, they only serve to stir in us a longing to be with our Father in His home.

In the heavenly city, "the tabernacle of God is **with** men, and He will dwell **with** them." Truly, heaven is a realm where man is at home with God. There is no need to go to a temple to approach God's presence, for He is always at hand. John says, "I saw no temple in it, for the Lord God Almighty and the Lamb are its temple." Neither is there ever a moment when one is not bathed in the glory of His presence. "The city had no need of the sun or of the moon to shine in it, for the glory of God illuminated it. The Lamb *is* its light." And, "there shall be no night there" (Rev. 21:22-23, 25).

The reason we will be so happy in heaven is simply because God is there. His continual presence accounts for our blessedness in the heavenly realm. Much more than an earthly grandmother who hugs you, feeds you, and dries your tears, the presence of our heavenly Father means utter happiness, joy, and peace. There is no death, sorrow, crying, or pain because God is present, and He will wipe away every tear (Rev. 21:4).

## ONLY THE HOLY

I performed a wedding ceremony for two young friends not long ago. Lorenzo and Anna had met at an American college. In time their love grew, and few who knew them were surprised by the announcement of their engagement. But the marriage would not be a simple process. Lorenzo was from Italy. In order to legally marry an American citizen and reside in the United States, he would have to meet U.S. immigration requirements. There was an incredible amount of red tape. Lorenzo was even required to stay in Italy for several long months before his visa was approved. Extraordinary measures of patience and perseverance were necessary just to get to a point when the wedding day could be planned. But the young couple's commitment to one another was strengthened through their time of separation, and eventually the wedding day came. Before the ceremony, friends asked both bride and groom, "Are you nervous?" And both Lorenzo and Anna gave essentially the same response: "No. I'm not nervous. I'm ready."

Heaven is a place for those who have persevered to prepare themselves for their spiritual wedding day. They have *pursued holiness*, "without which no one will see the Lord" (Heb. 12:14). In Revelation 21:2, "the **Holy** City, New Jerusalem" is "**prepared** as a bride" (Rev. 21:2, cf. 21:10). She is *ready*, because she is *holy*. No aspect of that city is defiled or unclean. Its blessedness, therefore, can only be experienced by those who are holy themselves. Heaven is truly a prepared place for a prepared people.

In heaven, the first earth has passed away, and God will "make all things new" (Rev. 21:1, 5). The new heaven and earth are new because everything there is ***right!*** Righteousness dwells there (cf. 21:1, 5; 2 Pet. 3:13). And, "There shall by no means enter it anything that defiles, or causes an abomination or a lie" (Rev. 21:27).

John also observes that "there was no more sea" (Rev. 21:1). In the book of Revelation, the "sea" often symbolizes corrupt human society. From it, an awful beast arises to make war with the saints (Rev. 13:1-7); this most certainly represents Satan's use of the Roman Empire as a tool to oppress Christians. The *sea* in Revelation is an object of God's punishment; its inhabitants are among those who consorted with the Great Harlot who persecuted God's people (Rev. 8:8-9; 12:12; 16:3; 18:17-21). When John looks at the holy city, the wicked sea of human degradation and corruption isn't visible. It just isn't there. The implication is that it is not possible for the unrighteous to enter heaven. If they did, it would not be heaven; it would be no different from the first heaven and the first earth.

While it may be politically correct and provide false comfort to believe that nearly every departed soul will spend eternity in heaven, we must realize that heaven itself would cease to be heaven if such were the case. If those who have disrespected God's name on earth, disobeyed His commands, oppressed their fellowman, and lived for their own selfish desires were allowed to inhabit heaven, how would it be much different from earth? No, my friend. "Either the day must come when joy prevails and all the makers of misery are no longer able to infect it, or else, for ever and ever, the makers of misery can destroy in others the happiness they reject for themselves" (C.S. Lewis, *The Great Divorce*).

Only those whose names are written in the Lamb's Book of Life will have the right to enter the holy city (Rev. 21:27). That Book of Life is God's record of the saved (Exod. 32:32-33; Phil. 4:3). It will be opened at the Judgment (Rev. 20:12). The names written on its pages are those of saints who have overcome and have been clothed in white garments (Rev. 3:5). Those whose names are not written in it will be cast into the lake of fire (Rev. 20:15). In Revelation, this includes all those who worshiped the beast (13:8; 17:8) and anyone who takes away from God's word (22:19). It also includes, "The cowardly, unbelieving, abominable, murderers, sexually immoral, sorcerers, idolaters, and all liars" (Rev. 21:8a).

We are sometimes asked, "How could a person be happy in heaven knowing that lost friends and loved ones are in torment?" In response we might ask, "How could a person be happy in heaven if evil people WERE NOT confined elsewhere?" Listen. There is no one in this world who loves the lost more than God does. He gave His only Son to save their souls. He knows where they have chosen to spend eternity. He sends them there. They have no place in His holy presence. God's love and justice for all concerned will not allow it. The knowledge of this reality does not ruin heaven for God, and it won't ruin it for the saved either. Caught up in the glory of His loving and holy presence, surely we will be at peace in the knowledge that the inhabitants of heaven are those who are there according to the will of God, whose robes have been washed white in the blood of the Lamb.

## THE NEW JERUSALEM: THE PERFECT HOME FOR GOD'S PEOPLE

We are pilgrims on this earth. As more than one old hymn reminds us, this world is not our home. "For here we have no continuing city, but we seek the one to come" (Heb. 13:14). Like Abraham, we are waiting "for the city which has foundations, whose builder and maker is God" (Heb. 11:10). In the book of Revelation, John is privileged to be shown that city, and to paint for us, as it were, the picture of it in words chosen by the Holy Spirit (Rev. 21:9-10).

As we look at our painting of heaven in Revelation, we are struck with how often the number twelve appears and reappears in the design of the city. Reading through the core of John's word-portrait in the last half of Revelation 21, you can hardly help but notice it. The city has 12 gates, each made of one pearl. There are 12 angels at the gates, and the names of the 12 tribes of Israel are written on the gates. The 12 foundations of the city are adorned with 12 precious stones, and the foundations are inscribed with the names of 12 apostles; those who walk in the heavenly city will stand on a foundation laid by the apostles (Eph. 2:19-20; Mt. 16:19). The dimensions of the city are 12,000 furlongs square (1,500 miles), and the width of the wall is 144 cubits (216 feet). What we are seeing here shows us that heaven is spacious, strong, secure, stunning, and symmetrical, but mainly it shows us that heaven is ideally designed for the saints. Can you see it? Twelve! Twelve! Twelve! It's all about the people!

If you haven't seen it yet, let me explain. The number twelve symbolizes the people of God. The origin of that symbolism goes back to the Old Testament, where Jacob had twelve sons whose descendants became the twelve tribes of the nation of Israel; they were the specially chosen people of God (Ezek. 20:5). In the New Testament, it is surely no coincidence that Jesus chooses twelve apostles (Matt. 10:1-5), and that He promised them that they would "sit on twelve thrones, judging the twelve tribes of Israel" (Matt. 19:28).

In the book of Revelation, the number twelve plays a prominent role long before we get to Revelation 21. In Revelation 7, John sees a vision in which twelve thousand from each of the twelve tribes of Israel are sealed by God. In Revelation 12:1, there appears a woman with a garland of twelve stars on her head; she gives birth to a child who was to "rule the nations." This event appears to represent Christ being brought into the world through God's chosen people. So, the number twelve is used in Revelation in conjunction with images which symbolize the people of God.

*Can you see it now? Our Lord has prepared an eternal home especially for us!*

My family has lived in several houses over the years, but we have never had the opportunity to work with an architect to design that perfect home. We came close to doing that some years ago when a builder allowed us to pick from several pre-drawn plans and make a few tweaks in the design to suit us. When the home was built and we moved in, we found that there were still some adjustments that had to be made. We lived in that house nearly twenty years, and it met our needs more comfortably than any other we ever had, but it wasn't perfect. But our God, who knows our frame better than we ourselves, has prepared a flawless home just for us, where every need is anticipated and every soul finds comfort and fulfillment for all eternity. How we long to enter *the city which has foundations, whose builder and maker is God!*

## BEFORE THE THRONE: FOREVER IN THE PRESENCE OF A HOLY GOD

Not long ago, I was privileged to visit an exhibit of some of the works of Leonardo Da Vinci. There was a video presentation analyzing Da Vinci's painting of *The Last Supper*. Narration and graphics pointed out how the figure representing Jesus had been painted a little larger than those representing the disciples. His head is framed by blue light from a window behind Him. And as if that was insufficient to draw the viewer's eye to Christ as the central figure in the painting, all of the lines in the ceiling rafters and along the walls funnel the focus of the viewer's eye directly to Him.

A central feature in John's portrait of the heavenly city is God's throne. All attention is drawn to it, and all glory, power, and blessing issue from it. At the outset of the portrait of the bride it is "He who sat on the throne" who says, "Behold, I make all things new" (Rev. 21:5). Later, John affirms that "the throne of God and of the Lamb" shall be in the heavenly city, and the river of life will proceed forth from the throne (Rev. 22:1, 4).

In Revelation chapters four and five, John had shared with his readers his initial view of the throne of God and the glory that surrounds it. This scene is now brought over into the heavenly city, and everything that we see draws us toward the throne.

The One who sat on the throne was "like a jasper and a sardius stone in appearance, and there was a rainbow around the throne, in appearance like an emerald" (Rev. 4:2-3). Jasper and sardius are precious stones that are typically red and translucent. If you've ever stopped to admire precious stones in a jeweler's display case, you would surely pause to gaze in awe at the beauty of the One who sits on the throne.

And then there is an emerald rainbow that colors the expanse around the throne as if with a glowing limelight. Ezekiel sees a similar picture in Ezekiel 1, with a bright rainbow around God's throne, but "the brightness was all around it and radiating out of its midst like the color of amber" and the throne was like a sapphire stone (1:4, 26-27). Although the two prophets envision rainbows of different colors, the impression left on our minds is the same. Who hasn't stopped to stare in wonder at a rainbow as it shimmered in the wondrous mingling of sunlight and rain? When we view God's throne, we will surely stand in wide-eyed amazement at the marvelous sight.

The appearance of God on His throne is thus symbolized with objects of strength and radiant beauty, but there is also overwhelming power; John says that he beheld "lightnings, thunderings, and voices proceeding from the throne" (Rev. 4:5).

John sees symbols of God's omniscience and omnipresence as well. Four creatures, having six wings and covered with eyes, are before the throne (Rev. 4:7-8). Similar beings were seen by Isaiah and Ezekiel in their visions of God's glory (Isa. 6:1-3; Ezek. 10). The many eyes of these creatures are meant to impress the viewer of the scene with the fact that the One who sits on the throne is aware of everything. He is all-seeing. And furthermore, He is holy and eternal! The four creatures "do not rest day or night, saying: 'Holy, holy, holy, Lord God Almighty, Who was and is and is to come!'"(Rev. 4:8).

Overwhelmed by the majesty of it all, twenty four elders prostrate themselves "before Him who sits on the throne and worship Him who lives forever and ever, and cast their crowns before the throne, saying: 'You are worthy, O Lord, to receive glory and honor and power.'" (Rev. 4:10-11). These individuals appear to represent the leaders of God's people from all time. On our behalf, they are compelled by the glory of Him who is on the throne to surrender their power, allegiance, and praise. Will it be any different for us? How could it be?

Throughout Revelation, many glorious events occur "before the throne." "Before the throne" the prayers of the saints have entered into God's presence, and the new song has been sung by the 144,000 redeemed from the earth (Rev. 8:3; 14:3). "Before the throne there was a sea of glass, like crystal" which, in contrast to the sea of corrupt human society, seems to represent humanity perfected and purified in God's presence; here the victorious saints stand and sing the victory song of Moses and the Lamb as they laud the "King of the saints" (Rev. 15:2-3). "Before the throne" stand all the redeemed – "a great multitude which no one could number, of all nations, tribes, peoples, and tongues…clothed with white robes." And they cry with a loud voice saying, "Salvation belongs to our God who sits on the throne, and to the Lamb!" (Rev. 7:8-9).

To walk into that city through gates of pearl on a street of gold and to gaze at last on the throne of His glory will surely render us forever awed. As we stand before the throne, never again will we experience the slightest inclination to doubt the worthiness of God to receive our complete devotion, allegiance, and adoration.

## A Tree by a River and Eternity

At the beginning of human history, in the Garden of Eden, man's sin separates him from the presence of God and from the tree of life (Gen. 3:22-24). A cherub with a flaming sword prevents him from going back, and mankind is destined to trek forward through eons of history to the end of time itself before laying eyes on that tree once again.

The references to the tree of life in Genesis 3 and Revelation 22 stand like bookends at the beginning and end of the story of human redemption. Paradise lost. Paradise found. Death reigns from Adam to Christ, and then death is conquered by Jesus' resurrection and swallowed up in victory when He comes again. And so the redeemed walk freely through the ever-open gates of the heavenly city, past the angels posted at each gate, right into the throne room of God. And there is the tree. Can there be any question as to what the symbol conveys? Man has once again been granted access to eternal life!

As John sees it, the tree produces 12 fruits, cultivated to nourish the saved for eternity. And its leaves are "for the healing of the nations" (Rev. 22:3). Not only do we have access to eternal life, but every injury and scar of our earthly existence will be healed and all will be restored to the condition originally intended by our Creator (cf. Acts 3:21).

John also sees a pure river of "water of life" proceeding from the throne. In John 4:14, Jesus promised to give water which would become in those who drank it a "fountain of water springing up into everlasting life." Before God's throne, Jesus fulfills His promise and gives "of the fountain of the water of life freely to him who thirsts" (Rev. 21:6). "For the Lamb who is in the midst of the throne will shepherd them and lead them to living fountains of waters" (Rev. 7:17). "And the Spirit and the bride say, 'Come!' And let him who hears say, 'Come!' And let him who thirsts come. Whoever desires, let him take the water of life freely." (Rev. 22:17).

IMPRESSIONS OF GOD'S SERVANTS IN HEAVEN

As John concludes his description of the bride, he uses the final brushstrokes of his word painting to enable God's servants to see impressions of themselves in that fair city (Rev. 22:3-5). Like all else that he has conveyed to us, the picture is filled with symbolism. And here, the images themselves are not presented in great detail. Nonetheless, as we look at them, we perceive that life in heaven is filled with a sense of purpose, blessedness, belonging, and eternal exaltation.

- **God's servants "shall serve Him."** We will be occupied with giving adoring homage to our God in ways that will no doubt honor Him and satisfy us.

- **God's servants "will see Him face to face."** On this earth, "No one has seen God at any time" (John 1:18; 1 John 4:12). When Moses asked to see God's glory, the Lord told him, "You cannot see My face; for no man shall see Me, and live" (Exo. 33:20). God hid Moses in the cleft of a rock and allowed him to glimpse His back, but the full view of God's face was not revealed. Nor could it be. Jesus Christ came and declared God to man in human terms (John 1:18). But in heaven, with no veil of flesh between, the pure in heart will see Him even as He is (1 John 3:2; Matt. 5:8). And in that eternal moment it is likely that we will understand the meaning of the words *majesty*, *beauty* and *glory* as if we had no notion of them before.

- **God's servants will have "His name on their foreheads."** We will be clearly labeled as belonging to Him. This symbol was used earlier in Revelation to describe the seal of protective ownership placed on the 144,000 (Rev. 7:3). Jesus promised that "He who overcomes" will be "a pillar in the temple of My God, and he shall go out no more. I will write on him the name of My God and the name of the city of My God, the New Jerusalem" (Rev. 3:12). All of this conveys that God's servants will belong everlastingly to Him in the heavenly city.

- **God's servants "shall reign forever and ever."** What greater exaltation could any man experience than to dwell forever in the heavenly city and reign with the King of kings? (cf. 2 Tim. 2:12).

These are the watercolor images that give answer to one of the most urgent questions we have on this side of eternity – *What will heaven be like?*

## VIEWING A MASTERPIECE

An old two-man crosscut saw hangs in our kitchen. A family friend painted a panoramic scene on the saw blade that depicts my wife's home place as it looked when she was growing up. There is a farmhouse, a barn, an orchard, and horses grazing in the pasture. The saw doesn't get noticed often, but when it does, our minds can be flooded with reminiscences of Sandi's childhood life on the farm.

Do you have a favorite piece of art? Perhaps it is a masterpiece hanging in a museum somewhere, or maybe it is just a child's finger painting that you have displayed prominently on your refrigerator. No matter. It is your favorite for a reason. You identify with it. It means something to you, and on some level it is beautiful to you. It may well remind you of something you tend to forget, while at the same time helping you grasp what you have never understood. Such is the power of a picture.

This is the sort of spiritual experience each of us can have as we take a long look at John's inspired word-portrait of heaven. It is truly a Divine masterpiece. Make yourself envision every detail. See it with your mind's eye. Meditate on it. Let it draw you in. Picture yourself as one of the servants of God who dwells there. Gaze long and hard. Look deep. And if in your day-to-day life, you are ever made to wonder if the trials and tribulations of this earthly life are worth it, look again. This is home.

*I'm just a poor wayfaring stranger.*
*I'm traveling through this world of woe.*
*Yet there's no sickness, toil nor danger,*
*In that bright land to which I go.*
*I'm going there to see my Father.*
*I'm going there no more to roam.*
*I'm just a-going over Jordan.*
*I'm just a-going over home.*

QUESTIONS

1. Does the bride in Revelation 21 & 22 represent the saved on earth or in heaven?

   • Would you agree that much of language used to describe the bride could be used of both the saved on earth and the saved in heaven?

2. What is the connection between God's presence and our happiness in the heavenly city?

3. Why can't a person who is unholy enter heaven?

4. What is significant about the fact that the number 12 is so prominent in the heavenly city?

5. Could a person be happy in heaven knowing that lost friends and loved ones are in torment? If so, how?

6. What do the scriptural depictions of God's throne tell us about Him?

   • What words would you use to describe your feelings when viewing the throne scene in your mind's eye?

7. How does the tree of life figure into the story of human redemption? What is significant about its presence in the heavenly city?

8. How will God's servants serve Him in the heavenly city?

9. Why is it important to study and meditate on what the Bible says about heaven?

*Chapter Twelve*

# We are Being Prepared for Something Great

**Some concerned Christians went to visit a man** who had become lethargic spiritually. He had slowed beyond a snail's pace. He was no longer assembling with other Christians to worship. He had begun to develop close friendships with those outside – those of the world, who have very little interest in spiritual things and few thoughts about God (Ps. 10:4).

As you would expect, they tried to discover the root of the problem and offered as much encouragement as they could for him to continue His walk with the Lord. They even said something like, *"Don't let anything keep you from heaven."*

To their surprise, he blurted out, *"Well, what are we going to do up there? Float around on clouds and sing all the time?"*

That may well be one of the saddest statements I ever heard. I feel such pity and sorrow when I think about it. What a low view of the most majestic, glorious, soul-stirring place there has ever been; the only place worthy of the name HEAVEN!

He didn't just come out and say it, but I think I know what might have been left unsaid. Was he thinking, "Heaven is a terribly boring place, and what little there is to do there is something I don't even like to do. Sing to God a lot? Ho, hum"? Poor soul.

What a contrast those words are to these eager ones - *"Eye has not seen, nor ear heard, nor have entered into the heart of man the things which God has prepared for those who love Him"*

(1 Cor. 2:9). I realize these words primarily refer to the revealing of the greatest story ever told – the coming of God's champion, His Son, to rescue us from sin. But the climax of it all is heaven! It's tailor-made by God and breath-taking in its splendor. It's fitted to us, and we are fitted for it. It's a "prepared" place (John 14:3). The Bible says in Hebrews 11:16, *"...He has prepared a city for them."* It's prepared only for those who with excitement, and no sighs, and no traces of boredom in their voices rejoice and sing...

> *When we've been here ten thousand years*
> *Bright shining as the sun.*
> *We've no less days to sing God's praise*
> *Than when we've first begun.*

They think to themselves, "Ten thousand years and then ten thousand more; we get to stay here forever!" It's a place where nobody feels he has seen all there is to see and then looks over to another and says, "Well, are you ready to go home?" We *are* home in the place we've always dreamed of being, and it's where we want to stay.

## BORING? NOT A CHANCE!

Heaven has always been a place of activity, purpose, and grand enterprises. The inhabitants of that place, the angels, have always served God in whatever He asked of them. His will is always done in heaven (Matt. 6:10). Angels do God's work immediately, without reservation, and with great joy. They "get into" what God is doing at any given time. They are all about Him and are excited about our arrival there to join them in the service of God (Luke 15:7,10).

Think about it. These angels watched Deity put skin on inside a young woman's womb. The Creator was created. The Deliverer was delivered. They sat ringside for the most vicious fights ever against the devil, and his angels. And Jesus never lost. They witnessed the bruising of the old serpent's head at the cross. A death that brings life, that's captivating! And then they welcomed a victorious Lamb, of all things, as He ascended into heaven and took His seat at the right hand of God. Do we believe for a minute that they peered into all of that and then said, "This is sooooo borrrrring!" Sure, they had to wait to get to the end of the story before they ever "got it," but they stayed glued to every enthralling page (1 Pet. 1:10-12). The last chapter, when we arrive there (or is it the first chapter?) is yet to come. They wait for us with eager anticipation. Our dwelling places are being readied. And when we arrive, we will be primed and ready to serve God in whatever great plans He has for eternity. Heaven never has been boring and never will be!

But not only is it prepared for us, we are being prepared for it. We are being prepared for something great! And get this; God doesn't entrust great enterprises to just anyone. They must have servant hearts and proven character. They are *proven* before they are *promoted*.

## AN INTERESTING LOOK AT JOSEPH

Joseph's life serves as somewhat of a pattern or template for what we are discussing here. What a life! Joseph didn't know all that God had in mind for him, but it was very clear that God was all along preparing him for something great.

**He had his dreams.** First, there are the brother's sheaves bowing down to Joseph's upright sheaf. And then, in a second dream, the sun, moon, and eleven stars bow down to Joseph. While not really clear, the dreams suggest greatness ahead for Joseph. His brothers and his father interpreted them exactly as God intended. Jacob kicked it around in his head quite often, pondering its full meaning (Gen. 37:10-11).

I suggest that Joseph's dreams sustained him during the hardest times of his life. They meant *something*. And they meant *something great*. Our dream of heaven does the same for us! I may not know *everything*, but that doesn't mean I can't know *anything*.

**He had his training.** Can Joseph handle responsibility? Will he work hard and serve faithfully through all sorts of circumstances? Well, let's see. Joseph is one day going to rule a vast nation but how in the world do you learn to do that?  Well, it's like this:

- In the first semester you can learn to run a man's house (Gen. 39:1-6).
- In the second semester you can run a king's prison (Gen. 39:20-23).
- At last, you can be given authority over a vast nation (Gen. 41:39-40).

First a servant, then a ruler (who still serves); that's the way Joseph's life went.  Some of those circumstances were horrible for Joseph, but he always worked hard, served God without wavering, and always held on to his dreams.  At last, the day came when he was reunited with his brothers and saw his father face-to-face.  So will we.  What a moment! I'm always emotional when I read about it.  It just "gets to me."  God is never wasting our lives, no matter what might be going on.  He is always working toward good.

**He had proven character.**  I once was in the coal mining country of Virginia, and a brother in Christ, with his mountain-man dialect said of another man, "He's a man of character."  But he pronounced it more like "ka'-ract-ur."  I loved it and it stuck with me.  Indeed, God needs men and women of proven "ka'-ract-ur"  God has always demanded trusted leaders when His work is being done (1 Tim. 4:16).  Every Christian who leads and serves should know that his greatest contribution to brethren is *who he is* and *what he stands for*.  Moral failure brings public service in God's work to a screeching halt!  Even in the world, how many public servants never achieved the promotion they sought because sin shot them down?

Potiphar's lustful wife became Joseph's second pit.  The brothers threw him in the first one.  I don't know if she can be called a harlot, but I know she did what harlots do.  They seek their prey and go after them.  Proverbs 23:27 says *"a harlot is a deep pit."*  Joseph passed the test with flying colors.  Nothing deterred him in His service to God.  He was not a quitter.  He was good and faithful in every assignment given to him.  And he came to learn what we need to learn.  God uses setbacks, troubles, and tragedies to shape us and mold us into His character (Gen. 45:4-8).  It's just the way He does things.  One thing (good or bad) leads to another.

We are never promoted by God without first being proven. The Bible is very clear about two things: Joseph was being tested by God, and we will be too.  Read carefully, thinking about Joseph's life as God's servant and then your own.

> "Moreover He called for a famine in the land;
> He destroyed all the provision of bread.
> He sent a man before them—
> Joseph—*who* was sold as a slave.
> They hurt his feet with fetters,
> He was laid in irons.
> **Until the time that his word came to pass,**
> **The word of the Lord tested him."**
> (Ps. 105:17-19)

> "Blessed is the man who endures temptations;
> for **when he has been proved**,
> he will receive the crown of life
> which the Lord has promised
> to those who love Him."
> (James 1:12)

> "And not only this,
> but we also exult in tribulations,
> knowing that tribulation brings about perseverance,
> and perseverance, **proven character**,
> **and proven character, hope."**
> (Rom. 5:3-4 - NASB)

At Joseph's first pit, the one his brothers threw him in, it became very important for him to learn not to be bitter.  If he is, and it festers as the subsequent trials follow, can you imagine what Joseph will do to his brothers when He is ruler over all of Egypt and he sees them again?  He would certainly destroy them.  It's what they even expected (Gen. 50:15).  God couldn't have that. He wants to bless them through a man of great "ka'-ract-ur."

At Joseph's second pit (Mrs. Potiphar), his moral character is proven. In both instances he was being prepared. We are too. God is preparing us in the here and now for what we will be and do in the by and by.

To Potiphar's wife, Joseph called sin what it was – *"great wickedness and sin against God"* (Gen. 39:9). He didn't rationalize or compromise. He didn't try to lessen what it was by giving it a sweet name like "an affair" or "friends with benefits." He fled!

And when he ran, she snatched his coat, and then smashed his reputation. He lost his coat but kept his character. She accused him of making sexual advances toward her. How backward was that! "Hell has no fury like a woman scorned!" That's a gross exaggeration, but she was certainly fuming hot in her anger.

Joseph's reputation took a hit but not his character. And it landed him in his third pit - the dungeon of the king's prison (Gen. 40:15). I wonder if anyone said, "Did you hear what Joseph did to Potiphar's wife?" That hurts.

Here's something we need to know. Reputation is what men *say* about you. Character is what God *knows* about you. Reputation is what men say about you on your tombstone. Character is what God says about you before His throne.

It makes me wonder how many people have had glowing and wonderful eulogies, but God knew better. It reminds me of the words of a country music song called "Two Black Cadillacs." The storyline is that a man's wife and his mistress conspire to kill him and do (I'm not endorsing that!). For the longest time the mistress hadn't known about the wife, and the wife hadn't known about the mistress. They both come to his funeral in respective black Cadillacs. It was a fine funeral, I tell you. *"And the preacher said he was a good man, and his brother said he was a good friend. But the women in the two black veils didn't bother to cry. They took turns laying a rose down, threw a handful of dirt into the deep ground. He's not the only one who had a secret to hide. Bye, bye. Bye, bye"* (Writers: Carrie Underwood, Hillary Lindey, Josh Kear).

Don't work on your funeral. Work on your life. Work on your "ka'-ract-ur."

**At last, Joseph was promoted to something great beyond imagination.** The end of Joseph's life staggers my mind. Of all things, a Hebrew man is made second-in-command over all of Egypt! He will run and administrate this vast nation through its greatest prosperity and then its greatest crisis. He had been faithful over a few things but was then made ruler over many things. Sound familiar at all?

Was Joseph able to see all of this as he was being dragged out of a pit and then carried away to Egypt by a caravan of traders? I think that answer has to be "No!" The whole thing will later make sense when played in reverse but not while the tape was rolling forward. It will be the same with many events in our lives. Only in heaven will it make sense.

> *"And things of earth that cause my heart to tremble,*
> *Remembered there will only bring a smile.*
> *But until them my heart will go on singing.*
> *Until then with joy I'll carry on.*
> *Until the day my eyes behold the city,*
> *Until the day God calls me home."*
> ("Until Then" - Stuart Hamblen)

I profited greatly in reading the material of Steve Farrar on the life of Joseph and the providence of God. He asserts that Joseph would have had a hard time understanding why things were happening as they were. He says, *"He had never read Genesis. And he didn't know his Bible because the Bible didn't exist"* (God Built, pg. 76). Joseph was living what would later be written for our learning (Rom. 15:4). But don't forget, he does have his dreams. They mean something. Notice that I keep reminding you of that. We have a dream too.

Before we make the parallels to us as servants of the Most High God, let's review the points again.

- Joseph had his dreams.
- Joseph had his training as a servant.
- Joseph's character was tested and proven.
- Joseph was promoted

## REST, REJOICING, AND RESPONSIBILITY

Two parables of Jesus deal with the end of time and the kingdom of heaven.  They reveal that we will not be bored in the next life but instead with great joy will serve the One who has always served us.  His servants *"shall serve Him"* and *"reign forever and ever"* (Rev. 22:3-5).  We are first servants, then rulers who serve - and all of it *to* Him and *through* Him (Rev. 2:26).

Even Jesus, who was made like us, did not quit serving us when He went back to heaven (Heb. 7:25).  Luke 12:37 shows a master girding himself, seating us to eat, and then serving us. *"Blessed are those servants whom the master, when he comes, will find watching.  Assuredly, I say to you that he will gird himself and have them sit down to eat, and will come and serve them."*

Does it surprise us that He would feed us once we arrive there?  And feed us with a spiritual food that satisfies, yet keeps us hungry for more?  He always has.  That's vintage Jesus: a servant leader – eternally!

Now, in regard to our service there, I will set the text of each parable before you and then draw some thrilling nuggets from these rich mines.  I will strive to not press the parables to mean something they don't mean, but folks, they mean something.  And I am persuaded it's *something great*.

### *The Parable of the Talents*
### (Matt. 25:14-30)

[14] "For the kingdom of heaven is like a man traveling to a far country, who called his own servants and delivered his goods to them. [15] And to one he gave five talents, to another two, and to another one, to each according to his own ability; and immediately he went on a journey. [16] Then he who had received the five talents went and traded with them, and made another five talents. [17] And likewise he who had received two gained two more also. [18] But he who had received one went and dug in the ground, and hid his lord's money. [19] After a long time the lord of those servants came and settled accounts with them.

[20] "So he who had received five talents came and brought five other talents, saying, 'Lord, you delivered to me five talents; look, I have gained five more talents besides them.' [21] His lord said to him, 'Well done, good and faithful servant; you were faithful over a few things, I will make you ruler over many things. Enter into the joy of your lord.' [22] He also who had received two talents came and said, 'Lord, you delivered to me two talents; look, I have gained two more talents besides them.' [23] His lord said to him, 'Well done, good and faithful servant; you have been faithful over a few things, I will make you ruler over many things. Enter into the joy of your lord.'

[24] "Then he who had received the one talent came and said, 'Lord, I knew you to be a hard man, reaping where you have not sown, and gathering where you have not scattered seed. [25] And I was afraid, and went and hid your talent in the ground. Look, there you have what is yours.'

[26] "But his lord answered and said to him, 'You wicked and lazy servant, you knew that I reap where I have not sown, and gather where I have not scattered seed. [27] So you ought to have deposited my money with the bankers, and at my coming I would have received back my own with interest. [28] Therefore take the talent from him, and give it to him who has ten talents.

[29] 'For to everyone who has, more will be given, and he will have abundance; but from him who does not have, even what he has will be taken away. [30] And cast the unprofitable servant into the outer darkness. There will be weeping and gnashing of teeth.'"

## OBSERVATIONS

- The lord prepared to go to a far country. Isn't this Jesus going to heaven?

- He gave his servants talents (money) and expected them to work it and increase it. The talents were not *ability* but rather *responsibility*. The responsibility given to them was "according to their ability" – which they already had (vs. 15). He will never expect more than we have ability to do.

- The lord returned from the far country. Jesus will too at His second coming. This is the end of time on earth. It is the "last day" (John 6:44). Anything that happens after this will be happening in heaven or hell.

- The faithful servants were given more responsibility (vs. 21, 28). The reward for faithful work is more work.

> *"His lord said to him,*
> *'Well done, good and faithful servant;*
> *you were faithful over a few things,*
> *I will make you ruler over many things.*
> *Enter into the joy of your lord.'"*
> (Matt. 25:21)

Servants love to serve. To them it is the greatest joy and the greatest privilege.

- This responsibility and service would be *in heaven* since there are no more earthly days…only judgment and then being ushered to our eternal destiny.

If you are like me you are wondering, "What specifically will we do?" I have no idea. It doesn't much matter to me. He died for me. I want to live for Him. *"Here am I, send me"* (Isa. 6:8). I may not know everything about my eternal dwelling place but that's okay. Did Joseph know everything? No, but he knew *something*. His dreams offered an intriguing glimpse…even though all the blanks were not filled in. It will be good at the end. God promises it.

### *The Parable of the Minas*
### (Luke 19:11-27)

[11] Now as they heard these things, He spoke another parable, because He was near Jerusalem and because they thought the kingdom of God would appear immediately. [12] Therefore He said: "A certain nobleman went into a far country to receive for

himself a kingdom and to return.[13] So he called ten of his servants, delivered to them ten minas, and said to them, 'Do business till I come.' [14] But his citizens hated him, and sent a delegation after him, saying, 'We will not have this man to reign over us.' [15] "And so it was that when he returned, having received the kingdom, he then commanded these servants, to whom he had given the money, to be called to him, that he might know how much every man had gained by trading. [16] Then came the first, saying, 'Master, your mina has earned ten minas.' [17] And he said to him, 'Well done, good servant; because you were faithful in a very little, have authority over ten cities.' [18] And the second came, saying, 'Master, your mina has earned five minas.' [19] Likewise he said to him, 'You also be over five cities.' [20] "Then another came, saying, 'Master, here is your mina, which I have kept put away in a handkerchief. [21] For I feared you, because you are an austere man. You collect what you did not deposit, and reap what you did not sow.' [22] And he said to him, 'Out of your own mouth I will judge you, you wicked servant. You knew that I was an austere man, collecting what I did not deposit and reaping what I did not sow. [23] Why then did you not put my money in the bank, that at my coming I might have collected it with interest?' [24] "And he said to those who stood by, 'Take the mina from him, and give it to him who has ten minas.' [25] (But they said to him, 'Master, he has ten minas.') [26] 'For I say to you, that to everyone who has will be given; and from him who does not have, even what he has will be taken away from him. [27] But bring here those enemies of mine, who did not want me to reign over them, and slay them before me.'"

## OBSERVATIONS

- The nobleman went into a far country to receive a kingdom. That's precisely what Jesus did (Dan. 6:13-14; Acts 2:34-36).

- Upon leaving he gave them responsibility. *"Do business till I come"* (vs. 13).

- The nobleman returned from the far country, and there was an accounting before him. Does this sound like judgment day to you?

- The servants who were faithful in "very little" were given more responsibility.

- Once again, the greater responsibility seems to be given after the judgment, at the end of time on earth.

## BUT WHAT ABOUT REST?

Perhaps you are asking, "But doesn't the Bible say heaven is supposed to be a place of rest from our labors?" You would be right. It does (Rev. 14:13; Heb. 4:9-10). We rest from our *past* labors. They will have ceased.

But future labor does not rule out rest. Allow me to make an observation from my earthly life. I am an avid deer hunter. I love being in the woods and communing with the Creator. But in the off season, there is a lot of work to do. There are food plots to plant and maintain, salt licks to freshen up, tree stands to check to insure safety, brush cutting to keep roads from narrowing, and shooting lanes to clear. It sounds like a lot of work, and it is, but I absolutely love the doing of it, and I feel at peace and rest as I do. I am in my element with the things I love all around me. A major part of heaven's rest is being free from temptation, sin, and its consequences: stress, pain, sorrow, and whatever else has burdened us here below.

And don't forget this major piece about heaven. We will not get tired – ever! It's the flesh that always gets tired here on earth. We can be standing on the rim of the Grand Canyon, getting covered with mist at Niagara falls, or lying on our backs on a star-studded night. But inevitably, even though greatly desiring to keep on gazing, at some point we give in to fatigue and simply must quit. But not in heaven! In heaven we will not be flesh and blood (1 Cor. 15:50-54). We will have spiritual, heavenly bodies just like Jesus that are released from their weaknesses (Rom. 8:23; Phil. 3:20-21).

Yes, after six days of creation, God "rested" on the seventh day but it doesn't mean He was tired. He just ceased from His creation activity. And then He moved on to other work. God never grows faint, nor weary. In heaven neither will we (Isa. 40:28,31). What a grand realization! Here below, we must sleep to wash away the fatigue of the day. In heaven, we will not. God doesn't sleep, and neither will we (Ps. 121:4). There's no night there (Rev. 22:5).

So, what are we seeing about heaven? We are servants there whose greatest joy has *always* been to serve God. We have stayed busy working for Him and are happy about anything and everything we can do in His service. Therefore, He gives us more and this time we will have unlimited and unfailing strength in which to do it. We are totally and completely at rest with our Lord and the greatest people who ever lived, and we never have to say goodbye. Let me rub my arms. I've got chill bumps!

Don't you wanna go to that land? Let's do it. Hold on to the dream. Do I hear singing?

## QUESTIONS

1. What evidence is there in the Bible that heaven will *not be a boring place* but rather is *an exciting place* of service to God?

2. What did God do with Joseph before promoting him to be ruler over many things in Egypt? Would Joseph have been able to understand God's plan for him while things were rolling along? When would he be able to see God's providence in his life?

3. **Thought question:** Have you already had occasion to look back at certain difficult periods in your life and see great purpose in those happenings? Could you see it at the time it was rolling along?

4. In what ways does Joseph's life parallel faithful servants of God today?

5. In the parable of the talents (Matt. 25:14-30), what did the master do for the servants who had been faithful in their responsibilities? Was this extra duty before or after his return?

6. Likewise, in the parable of the minas (Luke 19:11-27), what did the master do for the servant who was "faithful in very little"? Was this extra service before or after his return?

7. What does Revelation 22:3-5 indicate that we will do in heaven?

8. What verses teach us that heaven will be a place of rest? Does this mean there will be nothing to do in heaven? Have you ever felt at rest in your soul even while working?

9. **Thought question:** Why should having powerful bodies in heaven be exciting to us?

10. **Thought question:** Do you feel sorry for the man in the opening paragraph who said, "What are we going to do up there? Float around on clouds and sing all the time?" Why or why not? Do you think that attitude will land him a home in heaven?

## Chapter Thirteen

# *T*he *Glorious Day:*
# When We All Get To Heaven

In front of the Shibuya train station in Tokyo, Japan, a bronze statue stands. A lasting tribute to a loyal dog named Hachiko. A popular movie named after him simply calls him Hachi. The irony of the statue is that it is just as steadfast and immovable as Hachi ever was. Just like Hachi, it stays with eyes fixed toward the train station, still waiting...waiting for the master. Let me tell you the story.

*Hachiko was a golden brown Akita,
owned by a professor at the University of Tokyo.*

*But Hachi was more than just the professor's dog...
he was his friend.*

*Hachi was very smart. So, every day,
when Professor Ueno came home from work,
he greeted him at the train station.
And they would walk home together.
But sadly, one day the professor died at work
because of a stroke.*

*Hachi was given away, but he always
escaped to the station...
the train station where he had
always waited...*

*Hachi waited...*
*and waited...*
*and waited.*
*He waited for 9 years*
*until he himself*
*died too.*

From the time I learned of Hachi, I have thought of him. We have a lot in common. I totally "get it" with this dog. I feel the same longing and anticipation, for I too have been waiting every day for my Master. Hachi waits even though he is told by townspeople, *"You don't have to wait anymore. He's not coming back. But do what you have to do."*

Likewise, I just keep doing what I must do. Anything less shows dishonor to the Master, for it was He who said...

*"Watch therefore, for you do not know*
*what hour your Lord is coming...*
*Therefore you also be ready,*
*for the Son of Man is coming at an hour*
*when you do not expect Him."*
(Matt. 24:42,44)

Oh, I'm sure there are some out there who see my devotion and think, "Poor fellow. He's just like that pitiful dog. Waiting for something that's not going to happen." God told me to expect that from some folks.

*"...knowing this first: that scoffers*
*will come in the last days,*
*walking according to their own lusts,*
*and saying, 'Where is the promise of His coming?*
*For since the father's fell asleep,*
*all things continue as they were*
*from the beginning of creation.'"*
(2 Pet. 3:3-4)

Need a simpler translation? Here it is: "Move on silly boy. He's not coming back." But here's where they are wrong. I realize that Hachi's master wasn't going to return, but mine will! ***"But the day of the Lord will come as a thief in the night."*** No amount of time changes the faithfulness of His promise and His inevitable return (2 Pet. 3:1-13). Before He left, He said...

> *"Let not your heart be troubled;*
> *you believe in God,*
> *believe also in Me.*
> *In My Father's house are many mansions;*
> *if it were not so, I would have told you.*
> *I go to prepare a place for you.*
> *And if I go and prepare a place for you,*
> *I will come again and receive you to Myself;*
> *that where I am, there you may be also."*
> (John 14:1-3)

And, I might add, that angels promised He would return (Acts 1:9-11). In the meanwhile, I strive to live holy and godly, as I look for the day of the Lord and speed its coming. Oh, Lord come!!

## THE DAY OF THE LORD WILL COME

What a glorious day it will be when heaven's final train rolls in with the blast of its horn. There will be no mistaking it when it happens. A trumpet blast will reverberate across the sky - perhaps louder than the sonic booms I used to hear as a kid that always made me jump out of my skin. Heads will jerk upward and...there He is! Jesus. Heaven's doors have opened, and there He stands in the clouds arrayed in all His splendor. Previously, we could not have withstood the brilliant glory. But on this day, we can. Our bodies are incredibly strong (1 Cor. 15:42-43). As soon as the trumpet blasts, everyone's bodies are changed to eternal bodies. Any fatigue, pain, disease, or immobility the saints had just a moment ago is instantly gone. Literally, they have jumped out of their skin which was unfit clothing for eternity (1 Cor. 15:50). It happens really fast.

*"...in a moment,
in the twinkling of an eye,
at the last trumpet.
For the trumpet will sound and
the dead will be raised incorruptible,
and we shall be changed."*
(1 Cor. 15:52)

Perhaps roots are heard popping in nearby cemeteries, vaults open, and casket lids lift up. The dead, all of the dead, are rising. It may be that those who are saved and have been waiting are so overcome with the joy of His return they hardly notice that others are crying and some are looking for places to hide. It's not a great day for everyone (2 Thess. 1:7-10; Rev. 6:14-17).

Those saved by Him begin to rise off the earth. They realize this giant ball has served its purpose, and it too rejoices as the sons and daughters of God meet their Lord in the air to be with Him forevermore (Rom. 8:19).

This is why I think and write about heaven. For the saved, there's so much to look forward to at the great gathering of all of God's people. I am blessed with comrades who do the same.

## SOBERING HAPPENINGS

While I have been writing this book, I have also been writing another. I had no idea when I began these projects that this book would be influenced by my friend and co-author's battle with cancer, and the other book by a main character's massive stroke. Talk about sobering! Both men, in their attitude and spirit, keep me focused on heaven. I believe they both stay at the station looking for the Master. I don't suspect either of them will be away somewhere chasing a ball the devil throws for them.

By God's wonderful grace, at the present, Steve is getting good and clear scans and continues to load his schedule full of work for the Lord. He wanted this book to be completed as soon as possible. I sat down with him one day and reluctantly asked him what he wanted me to do with the book if he was called home before we were done. His simple answer was, ***"Finish it."*** I wasn't surprised. Finishing is a theme of his life (2 Tim. 4:6-8).

One night while lying in bed beside his wife Sandi, who was also struggling with her health, Steve said, *"The way we are going, neither one of us is likely to be around here much longer. I will not have you as my wife there, but I will have you as my sister, and I like that"* (cf. Mt. 22:30). She's not just any sister; she is the sister who helped her man through his battles and onward toward heaven. I know the feeling, for I have a wonderful wife (and sister-in-Christ) by my side also. It's all about family.

The other brother-in-Christ, who survived a widow-maker stroke, is my friend Eddie. Since his stroke, his eyes are also fixed toward the sky. His peripheral vision has been affected, but he's 20/20 straight ahead. Spiritually, that's where we all need to be (Prov. 4:25-27; Deut. 5:32-33). He knows that Jesus is one day coming on the clouds.

> *"For the Lord Himself will descend from heaven*
> *with a shout, with the voice of an archangel,*
> *and with the trumpet of God.*
> *And the dead in Christ will rise first.*
> *Then we who are alive and remain shall be caught*
> *up together with them in the clouds,*
> *to meet the Lord in the air.*
> *And thus shall we always be with the Lord."*
> (1 Thess. 4:16-17)

Eddie has called me many days and said, *"Hey brother, I see a cloud. It's a big cloud. It'll hold a whole bunch of us."* One day, he said, *"I see a cloud. It's a little one, but it'll hold me and you."*

I thank God for the "Hachies" in my life and look forward to meeting them all in the air surrounding the One who has always been the center of our lives.

## NOT A SMALL WORLD, IT'S A BIG FAMILY

Have you ever had a moment when you felt almost total peace and happiness? The feeling you will have in the clouds will surpass it beyond measure. The satisfaction is overwhelming as you look into the smiling face of Jesus, and you are now just like Him (Ps. 17:15). The embrace of the elder Brother will feel so good and the praise *of* Him and *from* Him is greater than any victory celebration you ever experienced. Admiration for Him glows on the faces of all the family (2 Thess. 1:10). He is beautiful, and all saved are beautiful.

This is the greatest reunion ever assembled. Excitement abounds because over there I see Abraham, David, Moses, Isaiah, Mary, Peter, Paul, Lydia, Tabitha, and more! Yes, I am convinced the Bible gives great evidence that we will know each other. There's David saying that he cannot bring his baby back to life, but he will go to the child (2 Sam. 12:23). I remember the night I watched an elderly sister in Christ pass away. As she came very close to "crossing Jordan," her daughter reached in her purse, pulled out a picture of her mother's little baby that had died as an infant. The aged saint looked at the picture, smiled, and crossed Jordan. And there are other passages that lead me to believe the needle points heavy toward the side of knowing one another in heaven (Matt. 8:11; Matt. 17:1-5; Luke 16:19-31; 1 John 3:2). We are heirs "together" of the grace of life and glorified "together" (1 Pet. 3:7; Rom. 8:16-17).

And up there are people Steve and I preached to long ago. They feel like a crown to us (1 Thess. 2:19-20). We are so glad they remained faithful until the end. There are brothers and sisters from across the United States and in places like Budapest, Australia, Zimbabwe, and South Africa. We were sad the last time we saw them and said goodbye. Life for us has been chapters of goodbyes. But now, we are struck by this thought. "There are no more goodbyes!" This truly is "awesome." That word is not over-used or over-exaggerated on this day. The best of all the nations are bringing their glory into the eternal kingdom, and we are full of awe (Rev. 21:24, 27)!

There are some we don't know, but just as we always said on earth upon meeting new saints, "Within a moment we feel like we have known them all our lives." That must be because the things that matter most, we share in common.

There are others there who were stabbed, stoned, mangled, mutilated, and cast away for standing with Christ...but you can't tell it now (Heb. 11:35-40; Rom. 8:18). They also look powerful. We are gathered to our people. To God, it's always been about the pleasure of family (Eph. 1:5). We battled through this world together, and now we are rewarded together. Soon, we will walk home together with the Master who pressed through this world, the grave, and the heavens - beckoning all the while "Follow Me."

## "THEY SHALL SEE HIS FACE"

Judgment is next, but for the saved it is an awards ceremony. He has brought His reward with Him (Rev. 22:12). The sweetest words ever heard are said. *"Well done, good and faithful servant; you were faithful over a few things, I will make you ruler over many things. Enter into the joy of your lord"* (Matt. 25:21).

Once inside the eternal city, we see God. Let those last three words sink in. **We see God,** the Father. It's never been done before - at least not the full exposure of His face - the full extent of His glory (Exod. 33:18-23). But now we can (Rev. 22:4). What will we do when we see the Father? I can only imagine. The singing has begun. We hear the song and strive to join. And joy beyond anything we ever dreamed possible is felt as we arrive there with our Master. The prettiest places we ever saw on earth pale in comparison to the beauty of this place.

Adding to that beauty now are the saints themselves. They are set on display there by God, and they shine forth as a lasting tribute to the One who made them masterpieces - little pieces like the Master (Matt. 13:43; Eph. 2:10; Gal. 1:22-24; Matt. 5:16). But they care nothing for themselves. Hachi was present for the unveiling of the bronze statue of himself in April of 1934, but he showed no interest. His focus was still on the master he longed to see. So it is with us.

It's all so wonderful. The angels themselves are taking it in - marveling at what God has done and the beauty of it all. No wonder it's called *Heaven*! God turns it all upside down and pours His kindness out on us (Eph. 2:7).

## AND IT DOES NOT FADE AWAY

We can't help but notice that the gates didn't shut as we entered the celestial city. And night never comes. Jesus illuminates the whole place. All of which spells SECURITY. We have so little of it here on earth. Sin messes it all up.

A short time ago, after a Bible study in our hometown, a sister in Christ stepped outside to her car. It was night, and there was little light in the nook just off a city street. As she approached her car, someone stepped from the shadows and spoke to her in an interested way. When she reacted with fear, he said something like, "Don't be afraid. I will not hurt you." I wonder about that! She ran with all her might back to the safety of the gathered saints. And the man eased away into the darkness.

Maybe this is why gates do not shut in heaven, and there's no night. There is complete peace, rest, and security. No one there is bad for you. No one there will hurt you. We shall always be with the Lord. And no one will ever defile it (Rev. 21:27). We go...

> *"to an inheritance incorruptible and undefiled*
> *and that does not fade away,*
> *reserved in heaven for you."*
> (1 Pet. 1:4)

Steve and I thank you for traveling along the pages of the Bible with us. We praise the God who invested all He has in those pages, and we continue to enjoy the daily journey. The aim of the pages we have written has only been to point you to the *Scriptures* on the grandest topic of all: Heaven! Our prayer is that you will think about Heaven and its Maker more each day, desire it and Him with all your heart, obey the gospel, and wait for the Master until He comes. We are going now to the train station to wait. Will you come with us? I see a cloud.

## QUESTIONS

1. Read carefully 2 Peter 3:1-13 and answer the following:

   In verse 4, what argument do scoffers offer for Jesus not coming again?

   What major catastrophe proved that everything has not continued the same since creation?

   What is said about the day of the Lord?

   Since that day is coming, what should we do?

2. List the wonderful things that will happen on the day Jesus comes again.

3. Will the Lord's coming be a great day for everyone?

4. As you think about the joy of heaven, what things about heaven are especially meaningful to you?

5. **Thought question:** A major point heard often to suggest that we will not know one another in heaven is the following: "If we know who is there, we will know who is not there, and it will cause sadness. Since there will be no sadness in heaven, then surely we will not know one another." Do you agree? Why or why not?

6. **Thought question:** Do you look into the sky and think about His coming as much as you should? What would doing this daily do for you?


7. **Thought question:** Is the example of Hachi inspiring to you? For your own private reflection, who have you known in your life that was a Hachi to you and motivated you to keep waiting for the Master?

# ABOUT THE AUTHORS

Steve Klein was born in Nancy, France, in 1958 to Clayton and Kathleen Klein. Steve has been occupied as an evangelist and writer since 1978. He and his wife Sandi have three children, Eric, Sommer, and Katrina, and two grandchildren, Clayton and Eden. Steve attended Florida College, the University of Colorado at Colorado Springs, and the University of Alabama where he received a M.A. degree in Educational Leadership. His preaching work has included travels to Africa and Australia, as well as numerous places across the United States. He currently resides in Athens, Alabama, working as an evangelist with the Eastside Church of Christ and serving as a Bible instructor at Athens Bible School.

Jeff May was born in Union Springs, Alabama, in 1963 to James and Glenda May. He and his wife Susan have two children, Bethany and Henderson. Bethany is married to Caleb White and they have one child, Garrett. Jeff is a graduate of Troy State University with a B.S. degree in Broadcast Journalism. He worked in the Television News Department of TSU until 1988. He then began preaching the "good news" full-time. He has since preached in Alabama and Tennessee, and currently is working as an evangelist with the Oakland Church of Christ in Athens, Alabama. He has traveled to preach in various places across the United States and Budapest, Hungary. He is also the author of *Hoof Prints to His Prints*, a devotional book for hunters, outdoor lovers, and people of the Word.

Made in the USA
Columbia, SC
03 June 2018